Dictionary for Our Time

To which is added a Dictionary for our Christmas-time

By Mike Barfield

Illustrated by Steven Appleby

Oldie Publications Ltd
London

This compilation first published by
Oldie Publications Ltd

The publishers would like to thank the respective copyright owners
for permission to include material in this volume

A CIP catalogue record for this book is available from
The British Library

ISBN 1 901170 00 4

Covers printed by Amica Fine Print Ltd
Text printed and bound by Woolnough Bookbinding Ltd
Design and production by Richard Adams Associates
Cover design by Steven Appleby

Introduction

A dictionary of comic definitions is an old idea. How appropriate then that this one should have first appeared where it did. It was written at the invitation of *The Oldie*'s geriatric powerhouse editor Richard Ingrams, following our collaboration on the radio series, *Beachcomber – By The Way*. Beachcomber (J. B. Morton) added a *Dictionary for Today* to his 1933 collection *Morton's Folly* and, despite the near impenetrable smokescreen of a new title (*Dictionary for Our Time*), some may still detect a faint similarity of tone between his efforts and mine.

My 'Dictionary' debuted in the very first *Oldie* on 21st February 1992 and appeared regularly for a total of forty-two issues. It should have been more but, sadly, I had already reached "M" before I realised I could stretch it way beyond twenty-six issues by simply sub-dividing the letters. Three addenda and a special Christmas edition also helped spin it out. Luckily, *Oldie* readers are a patient lot. Only one took such offence at a certain definition (included herein) as to suggest I be made the subject of some Western equivalent of the fatwah.

In preparing this collected edition of the *Dictionary* I have dropped some hopelessly out-of-date entries, revised others, and added new material - though it remains largely as it appeared in the magazine. Strangely enough, revising the text was a pleasant undertaking as it mostly involved striking out the names of now-vanished politicians. However, I would hesitate to claim *all* the credit for their going.

Mike Barfield, London, 1996

Acknowledgements

Our thanks to Richard Ingrams, James Pembroke, Nicola Sherring, Jessica Duncan, John Gibbens, David Ford, Harriet Docker, Emma Soames, and all at *The Oldie* past and present. Thanks also to the team at Richard Adams Associates. The author is particularly grateful to Marta and Giuseppe Pittarello in whose café the majority of this text was written.

A

Able-bodied Any person refused Invalidity Benefit is deemed to be able-bodied.

Aborigine Non-speaking character actor in Australian movies.

Abortion The Chinese method of birth control.

Abuse The motorist's greeting to his fellows.

Access 1. A credit card. 2. Court ruling allowing an estranged parent to take his or her children to the zoo on Sundays.

Accident Any negligent or malicious behaviour by a member of the Establishment.

Accountant A late twentieth-century moral arbiter.

Abuse

Accurate Adjective used to describe a newspaper article with more than half of its facts correct.
Acid House Impolite nickname for ICI's headquarters.
Acid rain Precipitate precipitation. The major British export to Scandinavia.
Acquaintance, Casual Any close sexual partner named in contested divorce proceedings.
Acronym The new language of Europe.
Action, Day of Inaction, Weeks of.
Actress The masculine form of 'actor'.
Additives, Food The sole cause of bad behaviour in children whose parents have no time to cook for or look after them properly.
Adult Pornographic.
Ageism The discrimination by the old against the young on the grounds of intelligence, taste, manners, and ability.
Airhead 1. US slang for an idiot. 2. US military flight chief obsessed with bombing foreigners (See 1). 3. See 'sex-doll'.
Agony Column The *Daily Mail* leader.
AIDS Illness said to be suffered by any unwell pop-star or celebrity who refuses to give details of his actual condition to the newspapers.
Alien abduction The removal of commonsense from most discussions about extra-terrestrials.
Allegory Any tedious film with a plot stolen from the Bible or some other philosophical work.
Amateur A person too stupid to profit from the talent they possess.
Amber Adjective meaning lager-coloured.
Angel Tabloid newspaper term. Any nurse not on a picket-line.
Apology The smallest size of type used in a newspaper.
Arbitrary Loser's assessment of any ruling made against them by a High Court judge.
Armageddon Shared erotic fantasy of both military advisers and anti-nuclear protesters.
Army Collective noun for British sports fans overseas.
Aroma Advertisers' term for the faint smell possessed by instant coffee.
Aromatherapy What most bag-people seem in desperate need of.
Arrest Hazard faced daily by younger members of the nobility.
Art, Modern Any painting or sculpture executed according to

principles developed roughly one hundred years ago.
Asexual Public claim made about their sexual orientation by discreet homosexuals.
Assembly Frustrating period for all home-build furniture purchasers.

Assets A model's breasts.
Assistant, Shop A paid observer.
Astrology Archaic pseudo-science by which intelligent people who don't understand how a microwave oven works seriously believe that distant lumps of rock control their lives.
Avocado A lavatory-coloured fruit.

B

B Identifying mark given to nuclear power stations e.g. Sizewell B.
Backlash Three letters to *The Times* complaining about something.
Badmouth Result of no longer being able to afford dental treatment.
Bag, Brown Paper Recyclable, environmentally-responsible wrapper for pornography.
Bail The small charge that criminals must pay to the court in order to get to re-offend prior to trial.
Bailey, Old A famous London casino.
Bald Archaic term, now considered vulgar. Preferred instead: trichologically-challenged or differently-haired.
Ballot-box An unusually-designed wastepaper basket.
Ban, Government A move by the state to boost the book-trade.
Bank Holiday A national automobile rally.

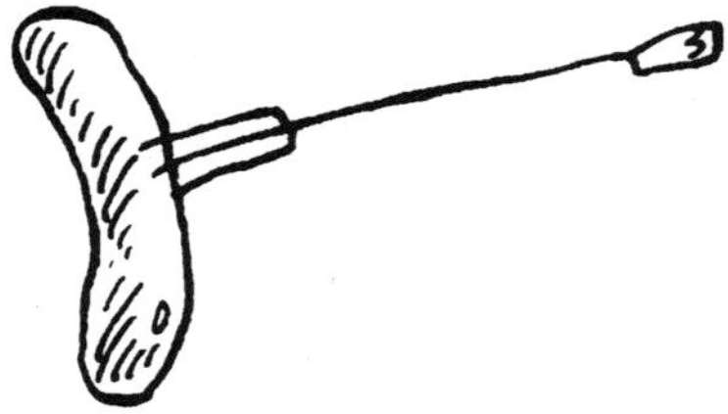

fig a – BEFORE

fig b – AFTER

Bankrupt Any company which runs out of other people's money is declared bankrupt.

Barbarism, Act of Any attempt to cut funding to esoteric arts projects.

Barmaid Archaic and sexist term for a Liquids Retail Liaison Officer (LRLO).

Baseless Any damaging allegation not yet proved correct is said by the allegee to be baseless.

Basic Model What the luxury version of a car reverts to after having its stereo stolen.

Bash Street The only British school still to retain traditional teaching methods and small class sizes.

Bastard Any person who causes one some mild irritation.

Barbecue Device for ruining meat outdoors.

Beagle A dog freed from laboratories by animal-lovers so that it can be locked up again inside one of their homes.

Beat That area of pavement that flashes past the window of a police panda-car.

Beauty-spot A wood with a car-park attached.

Bee A non-unionised food-industry worker.

Beep The welcoming tone of the telephone answering-machine.

Best, Sunday A person's least soiled jogging clothes or velour lounging suit.

Bible, The Any fully comprehensive

guide-book such as a car-maintenance manual etc.

Bimbo 1. Girl prepared to be seen in the company of newspaper editors. Traditionally thought of as stupid. 2. In more innocent times, a cute name given to a circus elephant.

Birthright, Englishman's Maternity Benefit, Child Benefit, and Family Income Support.

Black The only colour trendy fashion-designers wear despite insisting that everyone else should be in purple, green, etc.

BMX A corrupt acronym of 'Bicycle Moto-Cross'; not 'Bike More X-pensively' as popularly supposed.

Body Close-fitting one-piece item of underwear, created by Donna Karen. John Brown's earlier prototype failed to catch on and now lies a moulderin' somewhere.

Body-bag An ill-fitting military uniform.

Book A coffee-table adornment.

Boring Anything young people either fail to appreciate or cannot understand.

Born again Result of rewinding maternity home video back past baby's first appearance.

Box-fresh 1. Youth term for the pristine condition of brand new training shoes. 2. Old residents' term for any new arrival at Cardboard City.

Bread, Sliced The worst thing since unsliced bread.

Break-dancing What cheap high-heels do.

British 1. Euphemism for poor, inferior, or shoddy – as in British Rail, British Telecom, British wine, British justice, British economy, British Isles, etc.
2. Euphemism for superior, as in British history, British constitution, British way of doing things, etc.

Budget, The An annual government economic statement of such importance that children's television has to be disrupted by its broadcast.

Burn-out See 'portable barbecue'.

Buzzword Any word on which a 'Just a Minute' regular slips up.

C

C Trendy vitamin found in chemists and, it is rumoured, certain fruits and vegetables.

Cab, Taxi- A mobile debating chamber.

Cable television Technological breakthrough allowing the middle classes to watch *Sky TV* and stripping housewives without a dish outside to let the neighbours know.

Cabriolet Soft-topped car. From the French for 'easily broken into'.

Call-box, Public An advertising hoarding for prostitutes.

Call, Cheap-rate Description of any call made on someone else's telephone.

Camera, Polaroid Camera bought by men.

Campaign, Military A series of recruitment ads for the Armed Forces.

Capable, Highly Official description of any minister not up to his job.

Caravan A car-drawn home, always given pride of place at the front of any long, slow-moving procession of vehicles.

Carbonation Process that renders liquids drinkable to the young.

Carcinogenic Property of anything drunk, eaten, or inhaled that is pleasurable.

Card, Greetings One of the great paintings of the world, reduced in size and with 'Happy Birthday, Mum' written on the back.

Carefree 1. Drunk. 2. Sleeping around.

Carnivorous Morally outrageous dietary trait forgivable only in the pets of vegetarians.

Cash dispenser A weekend meeting-place for townsfolk.

Casual sex Now defined as sex for which one does not have to dress up – thereby excluding transvestism, S & M, and rubber and leather fetishes.

Casualty of War, The First Immediate loss of live television coverage.

Catalogue of errors See 'Hansard'.

Catchy Irritating, as in 'What a catchy theme tune'.

Celebration Word used solely in the titles of pointless and expensive gift-books, as in 'Pips! A celebration of the Greenwich Time Signal'.

Celibacy The brief period between any two acts of sexual intercourse.

Centigrade The temperature abroad.

Cereal A traditional English breakfast – for farm animals.

Ceremony, Wedding A pre-divorce necessity.

Certificate, Death See 'driving licence'.

Chairperson Correct term for any man or woman in a wheelchair.

Changeable How TV meteorologists describe weather they cannot predict.

Chaos Theory New theory invented by scientists panicked by the thought that the public were beginning to understand the old ones.

Charity A poor excuse for going parachute jumping in fancy-dress.

Charity Record A pop record that people charitably pretend is worth buying.

Chastity belt The area of land surrounding a nunnery.

Chattering classes Result of pupil's lack of respect for teachers.

Cheek Self-confidence shown by social inferiors.

Cheerless Newspaper term for a pensioner's Christmas.

Chorus, Greek Karaoke night at the Olympic kebab-house.

Church Quaint disused period building perfect for renovation into recording studios, unique dwelling spaces etc.

Churchyard A place where teenagers can smoke undisturbed.

Clamp, Wheel Ingenious device for rendering parked cars immobile.

Classical music Highbrow jingles used in advertising.

Clear conscience Short memory.

Climate, Current Euphemism for anything except the weather e.g. political situation, number of HIV infectees etc.

Closing-time A challenge to lager-drinkers.

Cloud-Cuckoo-Land A fiercely-contested political constituency.

Cold call 1. An unsolicited trade or business phone-call. 2. A phone-call made to the office to explain one's sudden absence due to '24-hour 'flu'.

Sufferers feel compelled to cough dramatically and pinch their noses shut whilst talking on the telephone.

Colonic irrigation Further proof that it's quicker by tube.

Colony Administrative area where the native population can still get away with blaming another country for their problems.

Coma A morbid trance-like state similar to normal sleep in that most people are brought out of it by the noise of relatives or pop music.

Comedian Anyone the police think is trying to be smart.

Common Rare or threatened, as in Common Frog, Common Land, Common Decency, etc.

Computer literate Synonym for between 2 and 18 years of age.

Concession Term used to make a forced climbdown look like an act of generosity.

Consumer terrorism The addition of dangerous materials to food by the public rather than the manufacturers.

Controversial Media term for one-sided, irresponsible, or ill-researched.

Cooking, Home M & S food microwaved at home.

Correspondence A series of complaining letters to dry-cleaners, the gas-board etc.

Crazy Every idea expressed by a character in an American film that '. . . Might just work'.

Counter culture The social, aesthetic and intellectual aspects of shopping.

Cream, The Cat That Got The The Cat That Eventually Died of Coronary Arterio-Sclerosis.

Creation An impractical designer costume.

Credit Debt.

Criminal, Convicted A private security guard.

Crop circles Skinheads and their acquaintances.

Crucified Losing six-nil in football.

Curry House Restaurant offering unlimited lager after-hours.

D

Daily paper Paper publishing corrections on a twenty-four hour rather than a weekly basis.

Dandruff Unacceptable clothing accessory, being white rather than black.

Day-glo Lurid colours found in nature – on backpackers.

Daytime Distinct period in the diurnal cycle, recognisable because the TV programmes are slightly better than those shown through the night, but much worse than those of the evening.

Deafness Sad disability in which sufferers are unable to hear traffic noise, portable stereos, and car-alarms with clarity.

Decay, Urban Useful process that helps make our countryside look good by comparison.

Deckchair Pioneering form of self-assembly furniture.

Declining years Time of life when one can successfully decline all invitations to dull events and parties by pretending to be too old and feeble.

Decorations, Christmas See 'Decorations, September to February'.

Dedicated Any employee unaware of his full holiday entitlement is said to be dedicated.

Deed, Good A watertight legal document.

Deep thought Process engaged in by the young when choosing training shoes.

Defeatist A fan of British tennis.

Delegate Anyone wearing a grey suit at the seaside.

Delicatessen Shop selling the worst parts of animals more expensively than the nice bits.

Deprived childhood A childhood without computers, videos, drugs, or pregnancy.

De rigeur French for 'I wasted money on this – so should you.'

Descriptive passage The dull part in a novel, thankfully lost in the TV adaptation.

Designer-drug Drug obviously taken by most of our modern designers, which has deleterious effects on eyesight and taste.

Detailed description What the police ask for to fool you into thinking they are then going to do something.

Detente Term implying a state of improving relations between potentially antagonistic countries. Curiously, the word comes from the French.

Devil Mythical evil being that used to drive people into church, and nowadays draws them into the cinema.

Devoted Any celebrity who visits his or her mother other than just at Christmas is said to be 'devoted to her'.

Diamond Jubilee Celebration of sixty years of not having your jewellery stolen.

Diana 1. Roman goddess of hunting. 2. British goddess of shopping, skiing and hospital visits.

Digital clock Timepiece accurate to one second a decade but impossible to read in daylight.

Dinner, three-course Triple-pack of M & S sandwiches.

Directory enquiries Proof that talk isn't cheap.

Dirty dancing Cromwellian view of Morris-dancing.

Discerning Advertisers euphemism for rich.

Discotheque A forcing-ground for mime-artists.

Discretion The boring part of valour.

Dish, Satellite TV aerial that blends effortlessly with domestic architecture by looking like a birdbath skewered to the side of the house by a drunk using an umbrella.

Display model The only one of an item left in a shop. It cannot be offered at discount because the manager is away.

Diversion An indirect approach to roadworks.

Divorce A post-nuptial agreement.

Docudrama A fictionalised reconstruction. See also 'Hansard', the tabloids, police evidence, etc.

Driving-instructor Usually the eldest in a group of joy-riders.

Drug-dealer The white-suited actor in a US cop film.

Dry-cleaning An offshoot of the wire coat-hanger industry.

E

E 1. Chemical added to food.
2. Chemical added to teenagers.

Eager to please All salesmen prior to signature.

Early bird Bird not dependent on public transport.

Early to bed A poor evening on television.

Earnings, Immoral All incomes in excess of one's own.

East Enders A harrowingly realistic portrayal of life on a film-set in Elstree.

Easter A national celebration of chocolate.

Easter egg An edible canister of air.

Eccentric, English Any Briton foreigners can't understand.

Eco-conscious Still awake after several minutes of a yet another rainforests TV programme.

Eden, Garden of An Old Testament theme-park.

Edible Word used to alert fools to the possibility of swallowing cake decorations, underwear, condoms etc.

Education, Sex The only set of lessons children can see as being still relevant to them after they've left school.

Effects, Special A plot-substitute.

Egg The chicken's contribution to political debate.

Ego trip A record-breaking journey made by Richard Branson.

Elbow-room Minimum space requirement of lager-drinkers.

Elder statesman Aged politician rightly revered for having got away with it for such a long time.

Election, General or Local Rare opportunity for parents to learn the location of their children's school.

Electoral register List of people happy to give their address to junk mail distributors.

Elevenses Brunch for under-achievers.

Elizabeth II The world's most famous State-supported parent of problem-children.

Elm Tree conspicuous by its absence.

Eloquent Description of any politician able to use an autocue.

Emancipation A woman who behaves as badly as a man is said to be emancipated.

Embarrassment of riches Tax avoidance difficulties.

Eminent Adjective available to professionals wishing to bump up their fees.

Employed, Self- Worker with uncommon regard for his or her boss.

Enamel Old-fashioned finish for teeth, now superseded by metal and plastic.

Encyclopaedias, Set of System for collecting dust in alphabetical order.

Endearment, Terms of The various clauses in any pre-nuptial agreement.

Endless nightmare The M25.

English as a foreign language American.

English Channel Convenient natural barrier to the spread of cheap alcohol and decent food.

Enjoyment, Pure A film despised by critics.

Entrepreneurial spirit Greed.

Ephemera Grandiose term allowing antique shops to sell garbage.

Epic Any film so unnecessarily long that one has to go out and urinate during it.

Epitaph The one bit of Karl Marx that people still read.

Error of judgement A High Court ruling.

Escort A prostitute with knowledge of the theatre.

Eskimos Indigenous people with no commercially-adaptable music and lacking in exciting new cuisine ideas.

Essex The taxi-drivers' homeland.

Estimate A rare occasion for modesty in workmen.

Etcetera Device used by journalists to indicate a lack of research e.g. 'There were many great deaf composers – Beethoven, etc.'

Ethnic cleansing The Euphemists' Euphemism. Unsurpassable.

Ethnic look Healthy, well-fed white people wearing beads are said to have an ethnic look.

Euphemism Word used by those without the courage to be crude.

Euthanasia A way of putting old people out of their family's misery.

Eve.

Eve The world's first victim of high-pressure selling.
Examination Unfair method of intellectual assessment biased in favour of cleverer and more diligent pupils.
Exclusive Expensive.
Exercise, Political Jogging display given by US President to refute rumours of ill-health.
Exit, No Sign placed conveniently by the shortest way out of a tube station.
Exodus, Mass The movement of people away from the church.
Expectancy, Life A home, car, video-recorder, foreign holidays, portable phone, second car, etc.
Expedition A trip to the shops.
Experimental Awful, as in experimental music, experimental train, etc.
Exploratory surgery Surgery to reveal the eventual cost of treatment.
Export A type of lager.
Express service Proper service compared to the speed of normal service.
Extinct Biological term meaning once-edible or once-decorative.
Extraordinary Anything ordinary as described by a children's TV presenter.

F

F Newspaper prefix to any row of asterisks.
Fabric of society Denim.
Fabrication, Total Insurance company view of all claims.
Face value The reward for investing in cosmetic surgery.
Fact-finding tour The long journey one undergoes in the attempt to locate a still-operating public library.
Fahrenheit Archaic temperature scale that had the pleasing effect of making the British summer seem hotter.
Fair game Newspaper editors' assessment of all public figures except themselves.
Fair play Even-handed cheating.
Fair-minded Obsessed with amusement parks.
Fairy-tale romance Story where the prince and princess live happily ever after, after their divorce.

Family tree Fascinating diagram showing distant relatives from whom one may one day inherit.

Family, Happy Family of no interest to TV documentary-makers.

Farce, Whitehall The apolitical pretence of the senior civil service.

Fare-dodger British Rail term for anyone who drives to work rather than swelling their undeserving coffers.

Farewell concert Often an occasion for false optimism.

Farm-house Country dwelling of TV celebrities, writers, sportsmen, etc.

Fashionable Any idea, practice or style specially designed to look stupid in a few years' time.

Fast food Food delivered promptly because it isn't worth waiting for.

Fast track Every number played at a 'rave'.

Fat lot of good Claire Rayner.

Favours, Sexual Bringing pornography back from the continent for friends.

Fawn Fashion term used to make brown sound trendy.

Fearless 1. Drunk. 2. Stupid.

Federal reserve Diffidence about a centrally-administered Europe.

Feelings, Mixed Drunkenness induced by cocktails.

Feet and inches Just two of the measures taken by Brussels.

Feminism Creed of equality, as a result of which women stand up for women, and men on buses no longer do.

Fence Politician's resting-place.

Fern Leafy plant growing wild in the foyers of modern office blocks.

Festival Any irrelevant public arts event funded by a council.

Fictional character The defendant as realised by police testimony.

Fiddle An instrument of business.

Fig The modern unit of concern for others.

Fighting spirit Vodka, whisky, gin etc. Also, lager.

Filing The systematic storage of waste-paper.

Fire-alarm Bell rung to allow employees to stand outside and smoke.

Firing line The hierarchy of redundancies planned in an office.

Fish and chips Meal unpopular with the young – being only fifty per cent chips.

Flame-thrower A bored British youth with the recipe for petrol-bombs.

Flashback Irritating cinematic technique used to reveal a character's earlier actions and the writer's inability to elegantly craft a story.

Flesh, Sins of the See 'World, News of the'.

Flight-bag Personal luggage with an above average chance of reaching your destination.

Flop A West End show with actors not known from television.

Floss, Dental Cheesewire for the gums.

Flying doctor Surgeon off on holiday to the Bahamas.

Folk music The indigenous music of the poor of many lands, now available on compact disc for playing in wine-bars.

Food additive Excess packaging.

Foolproof Any system which only intelligent people can ruin is said to be foolproof.

Forest A football team.

Forge ahead Road-sign indicating driver's proximity to Ye Olde Smithy Gifte Shoppe.

Forthcoming attractions Imminent disappointments.

Fortune-teller Mystic gifted with such amazing powers that they are always capable of gaining employment with a funfair.

Fox-hunting Still the most efficient way of ruining crops, frightening sheep, eradicating stray domestic pets, and annoying townies.

Fracas Elegant French term for a fistfight outside a boozer.

Fracture Clinic An après-ski venue.

Freedom of speech The inalienable right to have people find you mad or boring.

Freemason A police officer.

Frequent flyer Passenger with a growing interest in air travel disaster probabilities.

Friday night Friday from lunch-time onwards.

Frigid Sober.

Fuller figure Fashion writer's term for the next size up from malnutrition.

Fun Vulgar, crass or sad, as in fun food, fun-fair, fun holiday, fun drink, etc.

Fun-run Unusual event in which people run through city streets without police in pursuit.

G

Gadget, Ingenious Any device whose use will eventually recoup the time lost in figuring out how to make it work.

Gallery, Strangers' Seating in the House of Commons open to MPs' constituents, hence the use of the term 'strangers'.

Galore Very few – as in 'bargains galore', 'savings galore' etc.

Galvanised into action Threatened with redundancy.

Gamble To travel by public transport.

Garbage What the Americans call their rubbish and what we call their television.

Garbage in, garbage out 1. A computing truism. 2. British youth custody policy. 3. The effect of tides in British coastal waters. 4. The electoral system of Parliamentary democracy.

Garden of rest Garden concreted over to save on lawn-mowing.

Gas-leak Unauthorised release of gas company memos detailing further price rises.

Gas-ring A circular configuration of chat-show hosts.

Gate, Heaven's One of the few places rumoured still to employ friendly and welcoming door-staff.

Gavel How judges attract the public's attention, in addition to passing ludicrous sentences and revealing their idiot opinions to the press.

Gear-change Dull mechanical operation from whose tyranny the motorist has been freed by the development of the traffic jam.

Gelignite Yet another material now superseded by plastic.

General Correct term of address for any close relative of Saddam Hussein.

Generally speaking Specifically waffling.

Geneva Convention A free Swiss holiday for businessmen.

Gentleman Now synonymous with 'old man'.

Gentlemen's agreement A drug deal conducted in a men's lavatory.

Get up and go Helpful police instruction to the homeless.

Ghastly mistake House of

Windsor euphemism for the former Duchess of York.

Ghoul Term of abuse for any person who pays attention to badly injured people in the street rather than one who pays money to see them in the cinema.

Gift of the gab The provision of a company cell-phone.

Gipsies Itinerant folk that tow caravans along the roads and then wonder why people dislike them.

Giro-cheque A lager-voucher.

Giveaway Budget Budget so-called because it gives-away the true extent of the Government's panic.

Given time Never. As in 'the economy will come right given time'.

Glam-rock Another name for 'rhinestone'.

Glazier One of the few working people to benefit after the Poll Tax was introduced.

Glorious leader A jingoistic *Daily Mail* editorial.

Glowing report Annual Sellafield account of radiation leaks.

Go-slow Accelerated work-rate for British railway ticket-clerks.

Gold Card Credit card available only to ultra-high earners and pickpockets.

Gore, Kensington The result of running over a poodle outside Barker's.

Gorgeous Any topless newspaper model whose first name begins with a G is said to be gorgeous.

Gory details A full account of the action in any popular modern movie.

Graffiti Modern social art-form that makes cave-painting look sophisticated.

Grail, Holy Much sought after item of ethnic tableware yet to be the subject of an exclusive *Observer* Readers' Offer.

Granary bread Bread recommended as good for the bowels by doctors, and good for business by dentists.

Grand opera Choral music at one thousand pounds a seat.

Grandfather clock A clock nowadays often no more than thirty years old.

Graph paper The *Financial Times*.

Graphic novel Euphemism for an 'adult' comic-book. The term 'graphic' seems to refer to their explicit depictions of sex and violence.

Grasp of politics Taxation

Grassland Brixton.

Gratuitous sex and violence Sex

and violence demanded by the public rather than the plot.

Grave Elvis's cunning hiding-place.

Grave situation What bereaved Americans end up in if they reject the 'cremation option'.

Gravity Force acting on all bodies, to the delight of cosmetic surgeons.

Grease spot Colloquial term for an area dense with kebab shops.

Great man or woman A public figure yet to be the subject of an unauthorised biography.

Greater London London without Haringey, Brent and Whitehall

Green Party Social event eschewing the use of disposable cups and plates.

Grey area John Major's Huntingdon constituency.

Grim Reaper Alias taken by legendary serial killer with unusual agricultural murder-weapon.

Group therapy A way of further cheapening psychoanalysis.

Guesswork The sound economic principle behind the management of your private pension money.

Guided missile Fast car stolen by teenagers.

Guns before butter Britain's Third World trading policy.

Gunpowder Plot One of the few conspiracies yet to be linked to the CIA.

Gutted The disappointment felt by soccer-players and herrings.

H

Hackney carriage A police van.
Haggis Scots dish soon to be renamed 'granary-based high mutton fat and meat waste conveyor'.
Hail A precipitation of lead in Belfast, Bosnia, America etc.
Hair-raising story Fictional success claimed by baldness cure quack.
Half-pint A junior lager-measure.
Hallmark Damage caused by bicycle storage.
Halo Like the bowler, a now obsolete item of headgear.
Hammock One of the few beds people still might find it hard to jump into.
Hampstead Heath North London wooded area across which parents are loathe to let their children wander for fear of them meeting actors, novelists, arts critics, and media bores.
Hand to mouth existence Living on a diet of beefburgers.
Handcuffs, Golden A lucrative contract binding poor unfortunate businessmen to interesting jobs with massive salaries and numerous perks.
Handmade 1. A ridiculously expensive British object. 2. A ridiculously cheap Third World object.
Handsome Description of any hideously ugly male photographed in the company of a female Royal.
Hands-on experience 1. What sick and disabled followers of Morris Cerullo yearn for. 2. Unwarranted consequence for many women of travel in crowded lifts and trains.

Halo.

Hang-over Lager-drinking souvenir.

Hard lens Contact lens easier to locate when mislaid than a soft lens as it produces a distinctive crunching sound underfoot.

Hare Krishna movement Walking up and down Oxford Street with a shaved head and a cymbal.

Hasty decision Accusation yet to be levelled at the legal process.

Haul The insignificant quantity of drugs or ammunition collected as a result of some massive police operation is called a haul.

Haunting melody Clichéd suspense music always played during exorcism documentaries in an attempt to convince the viewer that some Catford semi is possessed by demons.

Head over heels in love Advanced intercourse position.

Headbanger 1. A long-haired, nodding rock-fan. 2. An unwary, poorly-anchored 'Hoppa' bus passenger.

Health warning, Government Proof of the ineffectiveness of truth in advertising.

Heartfelt thanks Gratitude expressed when employees accept redundancy without making a fuss.

Hearts and minds Finely-ground 'meat product' ingredients.

Heather, Lucky white Plant conferring good fortune on apparently everyone except those reduced to pressing it upon the public in the street.

Heavily influenced by Description used of any artist who steals the ideas of another.

Heavy metal Leaden music.

Hectare Charmless metric unit of area whose only resemblance to 'the acre' is purely anagrammatical.

Helicopter Remarkable feat of aeronautic design whose noble history begins with Leonardo and ends with Noel Edmonds and the Duchess of York.

Hell Concept dismissed by all modern theologians who do not travel by public transport.

Her Majesty's Stationery Office The country's leading publisher of horror and fantasy titles.

Heresy The notion that life would be better without television.

Heritage centre An elegant Portakabin facilitating the sale of mugs and T-shirts close to a national monument.

Heritage industry An opportunity for unemployed miners to pretend to be Victorian colliers.

Hermit Tabloid description of any

celebrity unwilling to be continually featured in the papers.
Heroes, Land fit for A graveyard.
Hibernation Nature's way of avoiding Christmas television.
Hiccup A long-term disruption to a public service.
Hideaway, Secret Royal holiday destination known only to the world's press.
Hidden agenda That covert, often malicious, ulterior motive possessed by an organisation, of which only a select few 'high-ups', conspiracy freaks and paranoids are aware.
Hidden benefits Little publicised social security allowances.
Highbrow Person who reads a novel before it is adapted for television.
Highlights, Sporting The blond streaks added to footballers' hair.
Hijack Potential aviation hazard useful for taking the nervous flier's mind off the possibility of crashing.
Hike A price rise
Hindleg Donkey limb at risk from exposure to politicians.
Hobbies Children's pursuits prior to the invention of video games.
Hoe-down A strike by agricultural workers.
Home from home Majorca.
Homeboy 1. A hip, US inner-city black fond of his local territory. 2. Salman Rushdie.
Homing pigeon Pigeon yet to be offered council accommodation.
Honey The allegorical representation of narcotics in post-modern readings of 'Winnie the Pooh'.
Honourable member Rare example of the amusing use of sarcasm.
Hook, Captain Seaman forced into criminality by Government failure to protect the value of Invalidity Benefit.
Hopeless case Legal action brought against the Establishment.
Hops Lager-flavoured plants.
Horror movies Michael Winner's home videos.
Horse-sense The Royal substitute for intelligence.
Hot The non-functioning tap in a public convenience.
Hot dinners Numerical concept never used in arguments with Roy Hattersley.
Hour of need Any sixty minutes of TV with Esther Rantzen.
Houses, Safe as Euphemism for any risky financial investment.
Human dignity Wealth.

Humble abode How people with two houses refer to their smaller property.

Humorist Dull writer incapable of having straightforward encounters with appliances, tradesmen and public servants.

Hump-back bridge Archaic and offensive term for a differently-postured crossing-point.

Humpty Dumpty Early innocent victim of egg-scare hysteria.

Hunger strike An attempt to effect change by going without food. Yet to be proven successful in Africa.

Hype One of the greatest – if not *the* greatest – nouns of the 20th century. A verb unlike any other. A word in a million. An etymological triumph. Unsurpassable.

Hypersensitivity Fear of large supermarkets.

Hypnosis The one way remaining to get people to do things without the offer of payment.

Hypocaust Early Roman attempt to add value to their homes.

I

Iambic pentameter Elizabethan attempt at the complexities of rap music lyrics.

Ice Age, New Newspaper response to consecutive cold days in February.

Iconoclast Self-description of any teenager who hates everything but owns a dictionary.

Ideal world Disneyland without entrance fees.

Idiosyncracies Faults in friends.

Ignorance No defence in law, unless you're a judge.

Ill-advised In consultation with solicitors or pension sellers.

Illegal substances EU ruling on elderflower champagne and warm egg custard.

Ill-fated Synonymous with 'invented by Clive Sinclair'.

Illness, Mystery More or less any illness confronting a GP with only two minutes to spare each patient.

Imitation leather Fabric chosen by life-revering sado-masochists.
Immaterial Facts which annoyingly disprove expert theory are said to be immaterial.
Immediate Eventual, as in immediate ceasefire, immediate delivery, immediate relief, etc.
Immigrant, Illegal See 'Immigrant, Penniless'.
Immobile Mobile 'phone after receipt of first call-bill.
Impact, Maximum An advert offending a huge number of people is said to have had maximum impact.
Impartial 1. Belgian. 2. Too foolish to recognise a bribe.
Impeccable references References concocted by the applicant themselves.
Imperial Term applying nowadays to soap and peppermints.
Impromptu performance Newspaper euphemism for any long-planned display imposed by egotistical performers on party guests.
Improved! More expensive!
Improvements, Home Getting the children to leave.
Inadmissible evidence Evidence that might make the police look stupid.
Inanimate object Animate object placed in front of TV set.
Inaudible The voice of reason.
Inbreeding Process discouraged in all beasts except Royalty.
In-car entertainment Entertainment that be can heard outside the car for miles.
Incarceration The jailing of the middle class. Working classes are banged up.
Incendiary device A *London's Burning* plot essential.
Incidental music Unnecessary music.
Incisive A TV interviewer who bullies his guests is said to be incisive.
Incompetent Due for promotion.
Inconclusive Said of any test with embarrassing results.
Incorruptible Independently wealthy.
Increasingly clear Phrase used by TV newsmen to indicate their slow understanding of the obvious.
Indefatigable Any fool who continues doing something long after it has ceased to be relevant or useful is said to be indefatigable.
Indefinitely How long libraries are closed for.
Independence The demand of young people to be answerable to

Index finger.

banks and credit companies rather than their parents.

Index finger Archaic term. Now renamed the video remote-control finger.

Indigestion Post-burger trauma.

Indirect taxation Ingenious method of acquiring revenue from children, pensioners, and invalids.

Individual portions Small portions.

Ineligibility Occasion for sadness among DSS benefit staff.

Inferiority complex An arrangement of buildings devoted to British tennis coaching.

Infinite wisdom Unending smugness.

Inform and Educate BBC policy, exemplified by *Noel's House Party*.

Informal talks Informal arguments.

Inhuman Human

Innkeeper, Jolly Innkeeper making huge profit from video games, juke-box, and quiz and karaoke nights.

Innovative TV term meaning 'impossible to understand', as in 'This innovative new series,' etc.

Insider dealing The dealings of city financiers whilst in prison.

Insomnia The result of worry over sleeping-pill side effects.

Inspiration Money

Intellectual property Houses in Hampstead, Tuscany, and Hay-on-Wye.

Intelligence, Counter Commodity shown rarely by shop assistants.

Intensive care Private health care.

Interval Concession made by modern playwrights to audience enjoyment.

Intimacy Sex.

Investigative Euphemism for rude or nosey. Thus, a Peeping Tom would be described as an investigative pervert.

Invisible man Man on bicycle in heavy traffic.

Ironic Any crass statement which causes offence is claimed afterwards to have been ironic.

Ishmael, Call me Archaic novel opening, now updated to 'E-mail me Ishmael'.

Isle of Man Soon to be renamed 'Isle of Persons'.

Isobar Line connecting areas of equal viewer confusion on hi-tech TV weather-maps.

Isolation unit The Sony Walkman.

Issues What politicians, being well aware of their personalities, would naturally prefer to fight elections on.

Italian parliament Roman political Drop-In centre.

Ivory trade Elephants for billiard balls.

J

Jack of all Trades Man paying heavy, multiple union dues.

Jack Spratt Early chlorestorol scaremonger.

Jack, Union T-shirt material popular with soccer fans.

Jackal, Day of The Novel outlining hard-line British solution to difficult Euro-politicians.

Jackboot Fascist footwear now worn by lesbians.

Jacket, Sports Jacket with paint or food company name emblazoned upon it.

Jackpot A libel case payment.

Jail Monopoly hazard, soon to be replaced by medical reports and community service.

Jam session A lengthy meeting of the EU Conserves, Preserves, and Pectin-related Foodstuffs Sub-Committee.

Jam, Traffic An encouraging sign

of continuing consumer investment in the automobile trade.

Jamaica? No, she went of her own accord as part of her 'Rastafarianism and the Shackles of White Imperialism' evening class.

Jargon The moron's dialect.

Jaundiced view Any opinion informed by reality.

Jaunty angle Angle invariably taken on last item on local TV news.

Jaw-bone of an ass The MP's lower mandible.

Jehad The Moslem version of that curious thing – the holy war.

Jehovah's Witnesses Religious zealots, called Witnesses because they wear suits, swear on the bible, and will answer any stupid question put to them.

Jackpot.

Jerry-built A corruption of German-built i.e. well made.

Jesus Christ 1. Robert Powell. 2. An expression of mild annoyance. 3. Charismatic Hebrew freedom-fighter who, rising above the stigma of disputed parentage and the lower middle-class tradesman mentality, led a campaign of peaceful non-co-operation against Palestine's Roman occupiers. Betrayed to authorities in a leadership power-struggle and martyred after public show-trial.

Jetsam Goods dumped and washed ashore i.e. crude oil, bales of hashish, boat people, etc.

JFK US president, now rumoured murdered by powerful conspiracy-book publishing interests.

Jiffy bag Envelope used to alert post office to damage opportunities.

Jigsaw Another picture the police would take inordinately long to put together.

Jingle Bells Song celebrating the delights of seasonal joy-riding.

Jingoism Failure to criticise one's country.

Job Centre London
Job Club Freemasonry
Job Week, Bob-A- Scout tradition threatened by EU minimum wage.
Jobbing actor Unemployed actor.
Jobs for Life Undertaker, gravedigger etc.
Jodhpurs Trousers that go with a Jilly Cooper jacket.
Jogging Exercise invented as an excuse for hideous clothes.
Join forces Imaginative careers advice to low GCSE school-leavers.
Jonah and the Whale Bible story now believed written by ancestor of Steven Spielberg.
Journal, Secret *Jane's Defence Weekly*.
Journey, Spiritual The long trip necessary to find the nearest working church.
Joyless marriage Marriage of couple without video recorders, theme-park trips, lager, etc.
Joy-riding A plea by youth for better public transport.
Jubilee line The Docklands Late Railway.
Judas Early victim of freelancing pressures.
Judo Sumo for anorexics.
Judy Famous battered wife who dropped claim to sausages in exchange for child-custody.
Jumble sale A sale of clothes that have been worn but not then returned to M & S.
Jump to conclusions Attempt by police to speed up the legal process.
Junk bonds 1. Premium bonds. 2. 'Moonraker', 'Octopussy', and 'A View to a Kill'.
Junk food What the EU does to keep up returns to farmers.
Junta The South American journal of new military writing.
Jury service Windfall earning-opportunity for ex-convicts.
Just for fun Just to fill time.

K

K 1. A salary unit. 2 Letter abused by morons in attempt to make sad businesses sound fun e.g. Kleen-a-Kar Ltd., Konkers NiteSpot, etc. See also 'Kwik'.

Karma Word used to mysticize peace of mind.

Keen gardener 1. Description of any actress photographed holding a trowel. 2. Person who actually visits a garden centre on a day other than Sunday.

Keeping Mum Ex-husband's alimony payments.

Keeping up with the Joneses Running up a large credit card bill.

Kent The Patio and Garage-Space of England.

Kent, Clark Journalist supposedly with super powers but yet to come up with lucrative Royal exposé book.

Kentucky Fried Chicken Rare example of a popular youth product being promoted by an aged, white haired and bespectacled, military figure.

Kept woman The result of hormone replacement therapy.

Kerb-crawler The Sinclair C5

Key to the door 18, 21, or five, if both parents are working.

Keyhole A low-tech personal surveillance device.

Keyhole.

Keyhole Surgery 'Small incision' technique invented by surgeons to reduce the likelihood of leaving the larger implements inside the patient.

Kick-starting the economy Making people unemployed.

Kid Pejorative term hated by children who want to be thought of as adults without actually behaving like them.

Kid's stuff Glue, cider, and tobacco.
Kidding, Just Kidding, only just.
Kidnapping The holding of people against their will. Illegal everywhere except airport lounges, supermarket queues, French motorways, etc.
Killer, Serial Low audience figures.
Killing fields The effect of intensive agriculture.
Killjoy Euphemism for unsafe sex.
Kilo Metric system prefix meaning 'not as elegant as the Imperial'.
Kindred spirits Two or more people with the same line in bigotry.
King for a day Now highly optimistic prediction about length of Charles the Third's reign.
King of the jungle Misprint for 'Sting of the jungle', the noted pop-singing environmentalist.
Kingdom, United Kingdom when asked opinion of the French.
Kinky Term used about any unusual sexual practice e.g. chastity, fidelity, etc.
Kipper Piscine victim of passive smoking.
Kit, Airfix The future of British aeronautical construction.
KitKat Two biscuit-fingers to dieting.
Kitchen Room where food is microwaved.
Kitsch Rubbish enjoyed by intellectuals. Rubbish enjoyed by lesser mortals remains rubbish.
Kiwi A Dralon-covered tasteless fruit.
Knife, Swiss Army Pocket-knife, to be replaced by the Joint European Whittling Utensil if funds are available.
Knock it on the head LA police arrest procedure.
Knockout, It's a Royal TV slapstick contest, now seen as rare moment of dignity for members of the House of Windsor.
Knoll, Grassy Dallas recreational space, popular with invisible gunmen.
Knot, Granny Hitch used to restrain residents in old peoples' homes.
Know a thing or two As much as one can hope for after years of modern schooling.
Knowledge, General Any uncorroborated but fascinating rumour about a person's private life is said to be general knowledge.
Koran The best-selling prequel to *The Satanic Verses*.

L

Labyrinth Tortuous path once leading to Minotaur; now ending in vacant Post Office counter-window.

Lacklustre British sporting adjective.

Lactation Handy secondary use for breasts too small to sell newspapers.

Ladybird Insect subject of socially-conscious nursery rhyme condemning absentee parents with children at risk from fire-trap home. The children are 'gone' – having been taken into care by social-workers.

Lambing time Occasion for overuse of sound effects in *The Archers*.

Lamentable Another British sporting adjective.

Lancelot The 'other man' named in Arthurian 'Royal Marriage Rift' stories.

Land, Open Land closed to ramblers by selfish farmers.

Landlord A Housing Benefit profiteer.

Landslide An election result.

Lane, Memory Street still safe to wander down at night.

Language, Bad Mid-Atlantic English.

Languish What Britons are said to do in foreign jails.

Lanky Term offensive to the Vertically Overcompensated.

Lapse, Memory Condition affecting defendants.

Laptop A computer occupying the same space when in use as a TV dinner.

Lark Bird seen rarely by the unemployed.

Last day! Everything must go! Open again on Monday with same stock.

Latin Language akin to English in that neither is taught in schools any more.

Latrine A bus-shelter.

Laughable Said of anything not at all amusing.
Laughs Last, He Who A TV critic, usually.
Laurel and Hardy US duo noted for ineptitude. See also 'White House'.
Lavatory seat Euphemism for an inner-city constituency.
Law-abiding citizen Citizen lacking opportunity for law-breaking.
Lawn A brown rectangle in the south of England.
Lean times The anorexics' journal of record.
Leap of faith 1. Changing your soap-powder. 2. Buying the latest hi-fi system in the hope that it will remain so.
Learn from your mistakes Poor principle to apply to health care.
Lease of Life, New Ditching your spouse for someone younger.
Lecture Lady Thatcher's small talk.
Leg over Career over.
Legal Process, Due See Legal Process, Slow.
Legendary Any musician who has not worked for years is described as legendary.
Legislation Laws hurried through to stop people benefitting from some loophole are known as legislation.
Leisure time activities Drinking and sleeping.
Leisurely pace The natural rhythm of British Rail.
Leitmotif Any irritating and hackneyed musical phrase repeated to the point of pain in a new musical.
Lemming Creature whose behaviour is yet to be explained by exam stress, credit card debt, or mortgage worries.
Lemon Fruit supplied with pub 'scampi' in clever attempt to convince customers that the dish bears some relation to fish.
Leniency Branch of law dealing with company directors and teenagers.
Lenses, Contact Worn by all those who wish modestly to hide their still being able to afford regular eye tests.
Leonardo A now distant historical figure – having been one of the Mutant Ninja Turtles.
Letterbox Receptacle for parcel-bombs.
Lettuce The prawn-cocktail's winding sheet.
Liability About the only thing most people won't accept nowadays.
Life About twelve years.

Life and limb Key Rottweiller objectives.

Lightning strike Strike planned weeks in advance.

Like you very much Coded statement of lack of interest in marriage.

Limited company What most actors and models prove to be.

Liposuction Costly technique allowing cosmetic surgeons to live off the fat of the land.

Listed building Building someone somewhere wants to pull down.

Lite An Americanism. The 'lite' form of 'light'.

Literally Synonymous with not at all, as in 'I was literally starving, literally broke', etc.

Litter Trade term for loose magazine advertising inserts.

Livelihood When threatened with its loss, any miserable job which the holder has hated all their life is said to be their livelihood.

Lively Holiday brochure euphemism for squalid, noisy, and dirty, as in 'This lively resort . . . 'etc.

Logic, Inescapable Logic, all too easily escapable.

Logo, Company Trendy vicar-speak for the sign of the Cross.

Lost youth Youth confronted with log-tables, books without pictures, simple questions about British geography, etc.

Lottery, National An excuse to show yet more balls on TV on Saturdays.

Lotus-eater Rust.

Love Sex.

Love of money The scenic route of all evil.

Low Countries Those at the bottom of the ERM.

L-plates Device for warning other motorists of golden opportunity for driving too close, flashing headlights, and swearing.

Lying low Escaped criminal on futon.

M

M Summertime traffic-jam prefix.

Made, British Badly put together in Port Talbot from parts manufactured in Korea, France, and Taiwan.

Made for each other Phrase now true only of Frankenstein's Monster and his Bride.

Magic Circle The M25.

Magnificat A premium brand of cat-food.

Magnolia A subtle blend of white paint and dirt.

Magnum force Champagne sales promotion team

Maintaining high standards Maintaining high prices.

Maintenance man A divorcee.

Maize DIY cornflakes.

Majesty's Pleasure, Her Jigsaw puzzles, it is said.

Make believe Signs of economic recovery.

Makeover 1. A radical hair and cosmetics overhaul. 2. A 90s lament. 'I useta makeover 40K,' etc.

Making allowances Benefit-book forgery.

Malcontent Person earning less money than his neighbour.

Male-bonding Sociological term for group lager-drinking.

Male organ *GQ, Loaded, Maxim, For Him*, etc.

Mall A place where tacky, over-priced goods are sold, leading down to Buckingham Palace.

Malnutrition The 'F-All' Plan Diet, popular with supermodels.

Mammal Creature capable of both suckling young and adding tap-water to milk powder.

Man of the Woods, Old 1. Rural victim of 'care in the community'. 2. A flasher.

Man or a Mouse? Are You A Sceptical child's question to rodent-costumed actor at Disneyland, Paris.

Mandate to govern Voted into office by less than half of the population.

Mangle Item of Post Office machinery.

Manifesto, Election Book published in the hope that few will actually read it.

Man-sized Persistent paper-industry gender-prejudice.

Marbles Recyclable glass game

played by eco-conscious children.

Marigold Former name of EU Bovine Unit BU 3201472/13Z (Dairy).

Marilyn Monroe A dead sexy actress.

Marquis de Sade French noble keen on inflicting pain, primarily through several execrable novels.

Married man, Happily Husband with mistress as yet unknown to wife.

Mars The god of chocolate.

Mary A woman of stainless virtue a.k.a. Mrs Jeffrey Archer.

Masculinity 1. Qualities the Political Correctness lobby deem boorish and unwanted in men, but applaud when shown by women. 2. A side-effect of lager-drinking.

Mask, Face Item worn by surgeons to reduce chance of positive identification in event of negligence charges.

Masochism A morbid desire to travel by coach.

Mason, Free Arrested mason after revealing his affiliation to the desk-sergeant.

Mass Observation Now known as 'Royal-watching'.

Massive savings Savings achieved by ignoring unneeded sale goods marked this way.

Maternity dress 1. A tight-fitting Lycra catsuit. 2. Paul Yates's everyday clothes (See 1).

Matt finish Perpetual fear of the *Daily Telegraph* editor.

Maybe The politically-deferred no.

Meal, Square TV dinner eaten during *EastEnders*.

Mean machine Railway chocolate vending-machine.

Measure of success Now clearly seems to be the metre.

Meat and two veg A burger and two packs of fries.

Meat, One Man's Is another man's animal-rights protest.

Media studies What students call watching TV and reading comic-books.

Medical records Longest UK wait for a minor operation, shortest time spent with GP, most expensive prescription etc.

Medium, Happy Fraudulent psychic after successful conning of yet another audience.

Meek Low-key social group cheated out of inheritance.

Meeting the needs of the Community 1. Slowly replacing all the amenities and services removed 10 years ago for being 'too costly'.

2. Providing lesbian only creche facilities.

Melting-pot Instant noodle-snack container after addition of boiling water.

Memo Term used to dignify any petty complaint sent around an office.

Memory for Faces, Good Useful gift for members of Michael Jackson's family to possess.

Memory, Test of No longer providing directories in phone-boxes.

Menial work Work done by foreigners and recent honours graduates.

Mental Health Act Act put on by defendant in attempt to avoid going to prison.

Merchant of Venice Trader constantly advertising a 'sale due to flood damage'.

Merchant, Speed A seller of amphetamines.

Merlin Arthurian magician who ended life trapped inside a tree. May explain Paul Daniels' fear of bonsai.

Messy divorce Every divorce involving children.

Met. Office Only office where staff are actively encouraged to sit and talk about the weather.

Meteoric rise The pay increase of any director of a recently-privatised company.

Methane Gas produced copiously by cows in their insane war against the ozone-layer.

Metropolitan Police Force Abbreviated to The Met to give more members a chance of spelling it correctly.

Mexican Wave Gesture of farewell to chances of ever repaying their massive US debt.

Mickey-take The money made from Disney's mouse

Microscope A credit-agreement reading-aid.

Microwave Oven invented just to prove that pub food *could* get worse.

Middle-age spread Fish paste or Marmite.

Midget Apparent stature of person responsible for designing new UK coinage.

Midnight, The Horn Blows at 1. Film with Jack Benny 2. Film about car-alarms.

Midsummer Night's Dream Plays under the name 'Donkey Love' in Scandinavia.

Miles better British attitude to kilometres.

Military intelligence Well-known contradiction in terms.

Milk bottle The courage required to still drink full-fat milk.

Millionaire 1. Man with soft-drinks pitch outside Madame Tussaud's. 2. A poor Italian.

Milton Keynes A university town happily free of students.

Minder A large, aggressive heavy thoughtfully provided to help prevent decent, honest people from accidentally coming into contact with pop-stars and celebrities.

Mind-set The full two matching hemispheres of the brain. (So far, available only in grey.)

Mindless violence Odd term used pejoratively as if to imply that premeditated brutality is somehow better.

Mineral rights Inalienable right of young to drink Coca Cola and Pepsi.

Mini-bar 1. Small fridge used to keep peanuts cold in hotel rooms. 2. Device producing incessant hum designed to drive hotel occupants to drink.

Minimum wage Maximum wage, as will be.

Ministerial position An updated entry in *The New Joy of Sex.*

Minority, Ethnic How one is yet to hear white South Africans described.

Mirage A sign of economic recovery.

Misalliance Cider and lager.

Misbehavin', Ain't Record avoided by ministers on *Desert Island Discs* for fear of later public irony.

Misjudged Judged.

Misprint Trade term for true fact in the *Sunday Sport.*

Miss United Kingdom What US tourists do at the merest whiff of terrorism.

Mistletoe Plant blatantly encouraging intimate behaviour at odds with today's sexual climate.

Mitre Hat that must be worn by bishops when operating machinery or handling food.

Moaning Minnie Disneyland 'cast member' annoyed by working conditions.

Mobile phone The thin line between conspicuous success and standing in the street talking to yourself like a madman.

Mobile home House built over old mine-workings.

Moderate Description of any right-winger in favour of hanging, but vehemently opposed to drawing and quartering.

Modern Euphemism for banal, senseless, lazy or devalued e.g.

modern art, modern marriage, modern farming, etc.

Moment in Time, At This The windbag's 'now'.

Momma, Red Hot See 'Hormone Replacement Therapy'.

Monastery Belgian lager-factory.

Money-lenders, Casting out of the Merely a forced relocation to new business premises.

Monkfish Snob cod.

Moon, Cow That Jumped Over The Cow suspected of steroid abuse.

Moonshine Technical term for light reflected off bottom exposed through car-window.

Morning sickness Breakfast television.

Morse Dull TV detective acclaimed as great intellect yet who takes two hours to solve crimes, compared to one hour for Miss Marple, Poirot, Bergerac, etc.

Mortals Be, Lord What Fools These People who go to time-share meetings genuinely believing they'll be given a TV set just for turning up.

Motherhood A career hazard.

Motivation Money.

Motive What the police attempt to find after failing to find the criminal.

Mousetrap, The Long-running play that if it contained swearing, sex and 'difficult themes' would have been loved by the critics and closed after two weeks.

Movers and Shakers The two types of East European car.

Moves in Mysterious Ways 1. God. 2. Rowan Atkinson.

Murder on the Orient Express And even worse conditions on Network South East.

Muses, The Nine Reduced to just four in attempt to cut arts-funding budget.

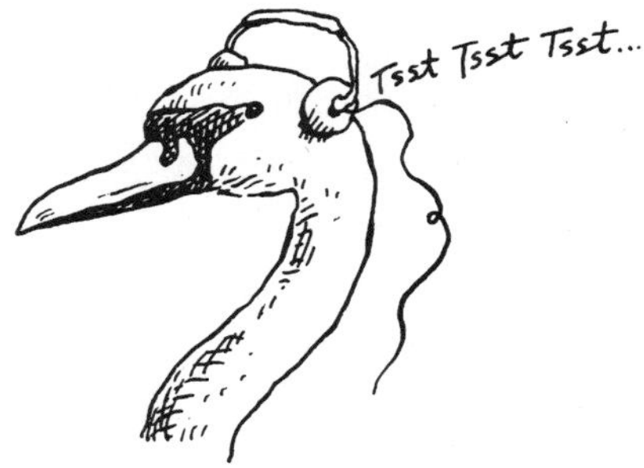

Mute swan Swan listening to personal stereo.

Mysticism An alternative explanation of life and the universe made by people still annoyed that they couldn't understand physics at school. As a result they all claim that 'Science has failed us'.

Mythical figure Zero inflation.

Myxomatosis God's plague on rabbits for their immoral sexual ways.

N

Naff Term used to judge something as outmoded or hackneyed, e.g.. the continued use of the word 'naff' itself.

Naïvety Modern definition of trust.

Naked ambition The desire to be a Chippendale or lap-dancer.

Narcolepsy Affliction on increase since televising of Parliament.

Nation Shall Speak Peace Unto Nation BBC motto at odds with the reality of Radio One.

National Anthem 'Here we go, here we go, here we go . . . '

National Curriculum Attempt to standardise UK teaching so that children end up being able to spell words like 'curriculum'.

National Front 1. Grandiose self-description of East London racist thugs. 2. The pretence that Britain is still an important nation. 3. The Page 3 chest.

Nationalists, Welsh Political group successful in having secured extra work for indigenous traffic-sign writers.

Native, Return of the 1. Thomas Hardy novel. 2. Home Office immigration policy.

Natural childbirth Giving birth in a fully-equipped modern hospital without resort to the conveniences on offer is described as natural.

Natural selection A gift-pack of Body Shop soaps and lotions.

Nature, Mother A battered wife.

Nature-lover 1. Briton with well-stocked garden bird-table and three pet cats. 2. Briton who worries about African rhinos and Amazon forests but would be hard pushed to identify an elm or a reed warbler or a slow-worm etc. 3. Claim always made by anyone who hunts.

Naturist holiday Holiday where loss of luggage by airline presents no great problem.

Nazi Anyone in uniform who annoys a teenager.

Necessary force Level of force unnecessary before things were allowed to get out of hand.

Needless to Say Verbal cliché used to make a superfluous statement even longer.

Neglect Now known as under-funding.

Negligence, Criminal The complete failure of prison governors to provide inmates with colour TVs, telephones, degree tuition, etc.

Neighbours, Good Soap episode which runs shorter than usual.

Neither fish nor fowl Vegan dietary credo.

Neo- Prefix meaning 'even sadder than' e.g. neo-Modernism, neo-Nazism, etc.

Neptune 1. Powerful Roman god of the underwater world. 2. A seafood pizza.

Nerve, Raw Tasty hot-dog ingredient.

Neutral Any country with too small an army to stand a chance of winning battles declares itself neutral.

New! Improved! Tacit admission by manufacturers that old product could have been better designed.

New Age Synonym for 'slow' or 'unwanted', as in New Age traveller, New Age music, etc.

New Man One who has read enough babycare books to really annoy women by telling them what they are doing wrong.

News, Yesterday's Next week's *Daily Mail* diary scoop.

Nicene Creed Early Christians' citizens' charter.

Niche-marketing The sale of things people don't want to the precise small group of people who don't want them the least.

Night-club Desperate attempt to make the Royal Astronomical Society sound trendy.

Nightmare, Your Worst A local planner's Dream Come true.

N.I.M.B.Y. Where Nicholas Ridley was buried.

Nipple count Scheme to encourage numeracy among *Daily Sport* readers.

No fixed abode Address given by Duchess of York.

No longer with us 1. Dead. 2. Listening to personal stereo.

Noah First person to claim to be conserving animals by locking lots of them up in a confined space.

Nomadic lifestyle Romantic gypsy term now applied to the movement of rich people by jet between their London, New York, and Los Angeles homes for tax reasons.

Non-entity A through-the-night TV presenter.

Nonsense, Utter What government spokesmen do.

Non-starter Current opinion of

the common prawn cocktail.

Non-stop entertainment What neighbours always enjoy loudly.

Normal behaviour Feeling that psychiatry is a con.

Northern lights The Blackpool illuminations.

Northern Line Line spoken by flat-capped actor in beer commercial.

Nose Pay through the The high cost of cocaine abuse.

Nose Up, Turn One's Instruction to cosmetic surgeon.

Not to be sniffed at Any perfume endorsed by an actress.

Nothing, Much Ado About Government line on any public health scare leak.

Novel idea An old idea written with more sex in it this time.

November the fifth The focus of a month's firework use either side.

Nudity Included in BBC TV productions simply to ease the burden of costume expense borne by licence-payers.

Number of the Beast Now changed to 0181-666.

Nurses, Doctors and Children's game in which limited pocket-money is divided unevenly.

Nutrient Chemical added to breakfast cereal to allow it to be sold as a food.

Nudity

O

O, Wooden Exclamation uttered by 'Baywatch' actor.

Oak, Royal Tree able to converse on equal terms with Prince Charles.

Objector, Conscientious A dead Iraqi.

Obligation, Moral No obligation whatsoever.

Obliging, Very Shop assistant working on commission.

Oblivion, Consigned to Minister sent to Welsh Office.

Observance, Lord's Day Watching TV on Sunday.

Observatory, Royal Tree bearing paparazzi in its branches.

Occupation, Reserved Restaurant critic.

Occupational hazard Redundancy.

Octet String quartet with job-sharing imposed.

Odyssey, 2001 – A Space Sixties film so far ahead of its time that even after nearly thirty years it still comes across as pretentious balderdash.

Oedipus Ancient Greek sadly several thousand years too early to appear on Oprah.

Off the Record 1. Any truthful revelation made privately by an MP. 2. Any lie made privately by an MP wishing to fool journalists into thinking it is the truth.

Offerings, Burnt Barbecued party-food.

Off-hand remark Judge's Islamic law ruling on punishment for convicted thief.

Officer material Nowadays denim rather than twill.

Official Synonym of dull, as in official biography, official history, official business, etc.

Off-road vehicle 1. Ugly, expensive jeep driven by brave young things not afraid to tackle the rough terrain of Chelsea. 2. Stolen car abandoned in country field.

Often, Do You Come Here? 1. Bad line to use on Salman Rushdie. 2. Question put to Fergie by resident Briton.

Ogle According to extreme feminist theory, what men do when not ignoring women completely.

Oh dear Phrase which police are

specially trained to deliver sarcastically.

Oil-fired Made redundant by British Petroleum.

Old Country, The Eastbourne and its environs.

Olympic Ideal Undetectable steroids.

Onan Patron saint of *in vitro* fertilisation.

One out, All out The Australian approach to dentistry.

Open all hours What shops now are, and churches are no longer.

Open verdict A lack of judgement

Opening night Final performance of any new Mike Batt musical.

Opium den A perfume counter.

octet

Opportunism See under 'initiative' in 1980s business dictionaries.

Oppressed minorities Those minorities yet to receive adequate representation on Channel 4.

Opted-out What people who die are now said to have done.

Optimist Person not up-to-date with the news.

Orange juice, Fresh A delicious suspension of fine-ground waste from previously-squeezed oranges in a mixture of water and pasteurised juice concentrate with added sugar and ascorbic acid

Ordnance Survey Map Farmers' guide to footpaths due for ploughing.

Organic farming Noble principle which due to cost merely ends up allowing a few rich people to be smug about their carrots and spuds.

Orthopaedic mattress Excuse given by hotel management for any uncomfortable bed.

Osmosis Scientific term which arts writers don't understand but use repeatedly in a vain attempt to sound educated.

Ouija Pseudo-spiritual game hit badly be declining standard of spelling.

Out and About What militant gays are proud to proclaim they are.

Out of commission London Transport euphemism for 'still to be repaired'.

Outdoor pursuits Police car-chases.

Overnight success Any artist or performer ignored for years by critics and then chosen at random to be praised. After twelve months he is declared a 'spent force' and allowed to quietly continue his career. After twenty years of obscurity he is then 'rediscovered' and hailed a 'forgotten genius'. He then dies and is described in obituaries as a 'sad recluse'.

Overpowering scent The smell of money.

Over-run What nice old movies and interesting documentaries never do into sports programmes.

Oxford Area Telephone Directory Large, unwieldy volume, now renamed *The Oxford Book of 'Phone Numbers*.

Ozone Gas destroyed by deodorant manufacturers to the benefit of sun block producers.

P

Pacific Ocean One of the world's great seas, soon to be renamed the Takeshita Corporation's Offshore Hydro-Expansion Zone.

Pack of lies Collective noun for journalists.

Package, Suspect Holiday arranged through bucket-shop travel-agent.

Page News, Front 'Sad Di Goes To Toilet Alone', 'Gazza Hazza Pizza', 'We Hype Sordid Book That Cost Us A Fortune', 'Stuck Journalist Rewrites Rival Paper's Scoop For Second Edition', 'Editor Falls For PR con-trick', 'Big Prize Bingo Starts Today!' etc.

Paintball Ridiculous 80s 'faux warfare' fad in which toadying employees could demonstrate their suitability for promotion by letting their bosses beat them hollow.

Pal Curious term of contempt used by pub psychopaths when addressing anyone they are soon to hit e.g. 'You lookin' at me, pal?'

Palace, Gin Queen Mum's name for Clarence House.

Pandora's Box Cardboard City house-name.

Panning for gold The lucrative business of newspaper criticism.

Panto The NEW super-detergent that makes your underpants WONDERpants! Buy some today!

Par for the course Any result or service worse than expected is said in this country to be par for the course.

Paradox What is now predictably described as a 'Catch 22 situation'.

Paradise, Fool's Necker or Mustique.

Paranoia The morbid suspicion that your psychiatrist secretly thinks there is nothing wrong with you.

Paraphrase Media-pundits' term meaning to remember incorrectly and then misquote badly the words of people much wittier than oneself e.g. 'To paraphrase H L Mencken . . . ' etc.

Park, Public Amenity open to drunks, drug-addicts, perverts and murderers, but from which dogs will soon be banned as being anti-social.

Parking meter Useful device installed to collect the revenue needed to pay the traffic warden needed to inspect the meters once installed.

Parson's Nose Can now be easily rendered the most attractive part of the turkey by simple cosmetic surgery.

Part With It, Oh, I Could Never Coded phrase meaning 'Make it ten quid more and it's yours'.

Partner, Sleeping Formerly a business term, now describes any close friend with whom one spends nights.

Pasty, Cornish Savoury snack which, under new EU food laws, will now only be allowed to be manufactured in large meat-product factories genuinely located in Cornwall.

Paternity suit Dark suit worn by defendant to impress judges at child support hearing.

Patient, Mental Anyone still expecting immediate treatment on the NHS.

Peak-rate A phone call made from work.

Pear Fruit yet to be described as typically 'woman-shaped'.

Pearly King and Queen Only British royalty for whom respect still remains.

Pease pudding hot Pease pudding liable to 17½ per cent VAT.

Pea-souper Thick fog curiously still associated by Americans with London rather than Los Angeles.

Peaty Whisky-makers' euphemism for foul-tasting.

Peccadillo Any indiscretion whose revelation does not force an MP out of office. If resignation results, it is described as 'a regrettable error of judgement'.

Pedestrian A motorist unable to park immediately outside his house.

Pedigree Chum A friend of Princess Di's.

Pencilled-in Any meeting yet to be cancelled at short notice.

People Who Need People 1. McDonald's 2. Those involved in chain-letter profiteering scams.

People Who Knead People Masseurs.

Per Cent, One Hundred And One What English sportsmen give just in order to lose.

Perfectly awful The most common form of perfection.

Performance, Royal Command Variety show requiring audience to believe that HM The Queen actually demanded to see Brian Conley, Roger Whittaker, Sarah Brightman, and The Krankies.

Perks 1. Those items small enough to be stolen from work without detection. 2. Affectionate nickname for BBC radio's Brian Perkins.

Permafrost TV's ever-present David.

Peroxide blonde Woman with a dark past.

Petition, Public A valuable source of Downing Street scrap-paper.

Pew, Take A Antique thieves response to finding church unlocked.

Philanthropist Term discredited by Robert Maxwell.

Photo-romance Princess Di's 'private' life.

Piano-tuner Man sent to sabotage Harrison Birtwistle concert.

Placebo Medicine that does nothing but still costs over a fiver on prescription.

Plaid Patterned cloth worn in

Scotland by Americans and in London by the Japanese.

Plain-song See 'Plane-song', the muzak played to calm airline passengers.

Planetarium Only place in central London that still gets dark enough to allow stars to be identified.

Plankton, Save the Little-known Japanese pro-whaling pressure-group.

Plant, Rubber Large factory producing much-needed latex.

Plaster of Paris Now with branches in Tokyo and New York.

Plastic surgeon Doctor with credit-card facilities.

Platform-shoes The scruffy plimsolls worn by railway staff.

Platitudes See 'Official Apology, Sincere'.

Play, Miracle Any non-musical that stays open in the West End for longer than three months.

Playboy Trade journal of US silicone industry.

Playful What dogs that maul children are apparently only being.

Playgoer, Regular 1. Person with company tickets. 2. A fabulously wealthy, incurable optimist.

Plonk Critics' term for wine ordinary people can afford to drink.

Plot, Essential to the Hollow excuse given for clothed scenes in pornographic movies.

Ploughman's lunch Chicken tikka and chips, chilli con carné, microwaved pizza, etc.

Plug 1. A chat-show appearance. 2. The only time a book is mentioned on television nowadays.

Plug, Three-Pin That one part of any expensive electrical equipment which is possibly still made in the UK.

Plumber, 24 hour Emergency plumber who takes a day to turn up.

Plummet A movement of sterling.

Plunder the archives TV term used to make repeats sound more romantic.

Plus VAT Found written in small print after every seemingly attractive price.

Plutocrat Ultra-rich Disney executive.

Poacher turned gamekeeper Poacher with hopes raised by reading *Lady Chatterley's Lover.*

Pocket-money The large fees paid to professional snooker players.

Point-duty Duty in which Jeremy Paxman delights.

Policy, Not Our Mantra chanted by shop assistants faced with customers seeking a refund.

Polite Society What our society used to be.

Political animal Rat, toad, snake, ass, worm, louse, etc.

Pony-tail Dated male hairstyle inviting comparison of the wearer to a horse's rear.

Pool, Indoor Pet in need of house-training.

Popcorn Last area of movie business where good taste is still a concern.

Popular Word meaning: 1. Cheap. 2. Tacky. 3. Easily understood by idiots. 4. Heavily hyped and advertised. 5. Destined to be out of fashion by next week.

Pornography See 'Art'.

Portable Any impractically large or heavy object made with a small handle attached is sold as being fully portable.

Portion, Individual Intriguing use of the word 'individual' as a synonym for 'small'.

Posse Brixton equivalent of a scout troop.

Possum, Playing Audience member indulging Dame Edna Everage.

Post-modernism 1. Intellectual excuse for parodying the past. 2. The attempt to update the Royal Mail by reducing the quality and range of its services.

Post-war Europe What it is hoped Europe will eventually become.

Pot, Gone to Student euphemism for trip to Amsterdam.

Poverty line '*Big Issue*, sir? Madam?'

Pre-marital sex Now compulsory test of future physical compatibility. However, results can be inconclusive, and the test may need repeating for many years before a couple finally recognise they are incompatible, and the man marries someone younger.

Pre-menstrual tension Anxiety of male partner over girlfriend's late period.

Pre-Raphaelite How sycophantic newspaper diarists describe any half-attractive young woman with long hair.

Pretty as a picture Euphemism nowadays for bloody ugly.

Price of Fame, The Phrase used by rich celebrities for no longer being able to shop unbothered in Woolworth's like all the lucky poor people.

Priceless Supermarket item bearing barcode only.

Primitive Any tribe yet to hear of Sting or Anita Roddick.

Princely sum Diana's divorce settlement.

Procedure, Necessary See 'Timewasting, Unnecessary'.

Profanity Known in TV and films as 'realism'.

Profit The money raised by lowering standards.

Profit, Gross The disgusting amount of money made annually by BT.

Profound What actors think they are being when they regurgitate idiot clichés about life very slowly. Deeply profound actors also nod their heads in silence afterwards.

Promised Land What the Palestinians were.

Promoter, Fight Lager.

Protest, Peaceful See 'Demonstration, Noisy'.

Q

Q 1. Much-missed Spike Milligan series. 2. The tasteless sign-writers' 'queue'. 3. The third syllable of Bar-B-Q. 4. The second mysterious initial in 'B & Q'.

Quack doctor Fraudulent physician, now described as an 'alternative healer'.

Quadraphonic sound A useful attempt by hi-fi designers to allow music-lovers to authentically and expensively recreate in their own homes the effect of somehow having managed to slip unnoticed into the middle of a symphony orchestra or pop group whilst carrying an armchair.

Quaint Term used by idiot US tourists to describe those picturesque signs of urban or rural poverty and neglect found outside their own country.

Quakers Spiritual movement with creed of respect, and non-violence, as exemplified by its most famous member, Richard Milhous Nixon.

Qualified Weasel-word used by con-artists to blur the massive difference between theory and practice, e.g. 'I'll have you know, I'm a qualified palmist/reflexologist/iridologist/astrologer etc.' Means little when the subject is hogwash to begin with.

Qualified success Nowadays, any graduate not on the dole.

Quality guaranteed Low quality guaranteed.

Qualms Secret fears only ever revealed by smug bores after things have gone wrong.

Quango Term used traditionally to describe any money-wasting State body other than the Government or the Royals.

Quantity, Unknown A quantity bought cheap at a car-boot sale with no questions asked.

Quarantine Strict period of isolation placed on all animals re-entering the country, with the exception of soccer thugs and neo-Nazis.

Quarter-staff Result of recession-imposed personnel cuts.

Quayle, Dan A former US Vice-Presidente. See also 'potatoe'.

Queen Mother Lovable Royal granny, prevented only by age from dancing on Wallis Simpson's grave.

Queen's English Queen's actually part-German, part-Danish, part-Cockney, etc.

Question of Sport 'Ampoules, capsules, or powder?'

Question-mark Bruise left on suspect during police interrogation.

Question-time, Prime Minister's Event curiously-named as the Prime Minister gets to ask no questions.

Queue, Dole An informal convention of small businessmen.

Quick See 'Kwik'.

Quick and The Dead, The The two categories of road-crossing pedestrians.

Quick-change artist A hyper-efficient beggar.

Quick-witted Slow-witted 'Have I

quarantine.

Got News For You' panellist after crafty TV editing.
Quid pro quo Latin for 'Cash on delivery'.
Quiet What all murdering, psychopathic neighbours prove later to have been.
Quiet Life, Anything For A Inquiry made of pharmacist about range of tranquillisers available.
Quill pen Elizabethan word-processor.
Quintessential Word used to describe the only decent piece of work done by an artist in a long and otherwise undistinguished career. It is said to be 'quintessential Smith,' etc., despite the mountain of rubbish actually being more representative of his or her output.
Quirky TV euphemism for any drama that was originally meant to be wildly amusing but instead just turned out to be irritating.
Quite Word used by waffling politicians to indicate a lack of any basis in truth for a statement they are making e.g. 'Quite a number of people feel as I do that . . . ' etc.
Quoted on the Stock Exchange The latest Essex Girl joke or that day's *Sun* front page headline. (These may occasionally be the same thing.)

R

Rs, The Three Previously 'de-emphasised educational concept', resulting in a generation that doesn't know its Rs from its elbow.
Rabble-rousing Pejorative description of any speech which provokes ordinary people rather than backbenchers.
Rabelaisian High-brow excuse for pornography.
Race-track Any straight stretch of road free of traffic lights.
Racketeer The 'astute businessman' of yesteryear.
Racy Publishers' code for those novels whose sex scenes end coyly in three dots rather than in graphic description, the latter being called 'raunchy'.
Radiant Tabloid description of any pregnant celebrity not actually pictured throwing up.
Radiator Domestic device for

producing loud knocking sounds from lukewarm water.
Radical Political euphemism for any new government legislation even more disastrous than expected.

Radiotherapy Speaking to the psycho-sexual counsellor on the local radio phone-in.
Rail To complain loudly and angrily, hence the association with train travel.
Rail-strike A near-imperceptible alteration to the network's now much-reduced services.
Rake's Progress, The Hogarthian early example of the use of the term 'progress' to imply a decline in the quality of life.
Rambo Violent US action figure portrayed on screen by Sylvester Stallone, and – curiously – used now as a general name for any vigilante member of the public, rather than any wooden film actor.
Random breath-testing The totally arbitrary stopping of young black motorists by the police.
Rangefinder Company that locates secondhand Agas.
Rank 1. The provenance of most British films of the fifties. 2. The quality of most British films today.
Ransom, King's A large amount of money e.g. that to be made from a reveal-all Royal scandal book.
Ransom note A valiant attempt by the criminal fraternity to keep alive the art of letter-writing.
Rap Repetitive youth music form. One of the few instances today of young people speaking loudly and emphatically, and yet you still can't understand what they are saying.
Rape of the countryside Oilseed rape, the yellow peril.
Rare species Zoo-goers.
Rate of exchange The high speed at which sterling is dumped in favour of other currencies.
Ration-book The last book many Britons got all the way through.
Rational behaviour The complete avoidance of psychiatrists.
Rationalization Euphemism for throwing loyal long-standing employees onto the dole. Curiously,

their jobs are usually then tendered to outside contractors who perform them more expensively and less well.

Razor, Occam's The dictum that the simplest explanation of any given situation is of no interest to conspiracy theorists or students of the paranormal.

Reader, I married him Proof, if it were needed, that *Jane Eyre* is a Victorian novel.

Reading-room Another euphemism for the lavatory.

Real life drama A type of TV programme.

Rebel What the millions of young people who dress in black leather jacket and denim jeans think they are.

Reckoning, Day of April 5th, unless deferred due to appeal.

Recognised authority How the media describe any bore whose field is too dull or obscure for any other sane person to have bothered taking an interest in it.

Recollections Word essential to include in the subtitle of any privately-published oldie memoirs with mystifying titles e.g. '"Muffins, Missus?" – Recollections of a Career in the Morning Goods Retail Trade', or '"Goosefat and Sticking Plasters" – Recollections of a Nottinghamshire Boyhood', etc.

Recommended Reading Credit agreement small-print.

Recommended Retail Price A mythical exorbitant figure plucked out of the air by manufacturers to make the actual retail price of an article seem slightly less alarming by comparison.

Record, Police Highest fee paid to informer, slowest response to 999 call, worst ever clear-up rate, etc.

Red Route Formerly thought likely to be across the Rhine Valley and into Western Europe. Now a busy London road carrying traffic at speed past failing local shops.

Reduced circumstances Crcmstncs.

Reformation, The What Beatles fans still vainly hope for.

Refusenik Council resident who will not co-operate with rubbish collection rules.

Regal Of or pertaining to suburban cinemas.

Regular guy US male with adequate fibre intake.

Rehabilitation The process by which newly released convicts are once again made to feel part of society – the unemployed and homeless part.

Reiteration Excuse used by bores wanting to repeat themselves.
Relate to That, I Can Nauseating psycho-babble phrase, beloved of Americans, and used idiotically to express acceptance of any situation, no matter how mundane, e.g. 'A cheese sandwich? Yeah, I can relate to that,' etc.
Relatively cheap Cheap only by comparison with some other even more over-priced item.
Release, Press Any diary 'exclusive' claimed by every paper.
Relegation The shaming demotion of a soccer team from exclusive coverage on Sky TV to the less remunerative BBC and ITV.
Relevance Patronising educational principle whereby children study *EastEnders* rather than Shakespeare, graffiti rather than Latin, and play video-games rather than team sports.
Relief Euphemism for orgasm.
Relief party An orgy.
Religiously Verb meaning to perform any task with a frequency reminiscent of devotion to sacred duty i.e. every other Sunday or once a year at Christmas.
Reliving the moment Sitting in the lounge with the curtains drawn watching an out-of-focus video of your ski-ing holiday.
Remake Film industry term. A subsequent version of a movie with more sex and violence than the original.
Remark, Casual The friendly chit-chat of shell-suit wearers.
Remarkable Word used by bad impressionists to let the audience know they are attempting David Coleman.
Remarkable likeness Any effort by an official Royal portrait-painter that is even half-recognisable as its subject.
Remembrance Sunday Day on which *The Archers* is moved out of respect for the dead of two world wars.
Remind me again Polite coded phrase meaning, 'I've completely forgotten what you told me as I wasn't really listening in the first place.'
Reminisce What people in their twenties now do about the 1970s, amazingly enough.
Remote control Rule from Brussels.
Remover, Stain Any official 'inquiry' not independent of Government.
Renaissance man 1. Critics' glib description of any artist equally

mediocre in many different areas.
2. Kenneth Branagh.

Rendezvous French cliché for any meeting between two people at night in an empty car-park. Use of the word is now generally confined to TV dramas where it is invariably followed by the time being stated as 'something-hundred hours'.

Rendition Any song badly sung is described as 'the singer's rendition'.

Renovation, In Need of Slight Estate agent euphemism handy for describing Stonehenge, the Rose Theatre, Pompeii, Atlantis, etc.

Rent-free Just one of the many attractions of shop-doorways for the homeless.

Reorganization The movement of employees to new positions, such as standing in front of dole office windows.

Rep. Short for 'reprehensible' i.e. pertaining to salesmen.

Repartee The exchange of scripted ad-libs by comedians.

Repatriation The sensible principle of sending every Briton, apart from a few Welsh and Cornishmen, back to their ancestral nations.

Repellent, Insect Concrete patios.

Replay, Action A rare treat for broadcasters: the opportunity to have a repeat of an original broadcast within that broadcast itself. Wow!

Replicas How embarrassed middle-aged men insist on referring to their collections of toy soldiers and model aeroplanes.

Representation Name given to the defence of unemployed black teenagers by high-earning middle-aged white barristers.

Representatives, House of The Avon Lady headquarters.

Reproach, Beyond Any establishment crook now living in a country with no UK extradition agreement.

Reprobate Term used to excuse and romanticise the poor behaviour of offensive drunken old bores who happen to work in the media. Similar characters in other fields are known more plainly as bastards.

Reproduction Furniture so poorly faked that it cannot be sold as the genuine antique article – even to Americans – is reluctantly admitted to be reproduction.

Republic Monarchy-less nation of people democratically confined to reading gossip about other countries' Royals.

Reputable dealer Drug-pusher that can be trusted not to 'cut' his wares with inferior product.

Reputation to Consider, I Have My Line used by prostitute in rejecting a politician's custom.

Required reading Very little nowadays, apart from medicine bottle instructions and credit agreement small-print. Everything else is eventually adapted for television.

Reserved Every empty table in a restaurant where the waiters want to get home early.

Resign! Dennis Skinner's cheery across-the-Commons greeting.

Rest Is History! The Advertiser's clever slogan for marketing new snooker-cue supporting device.

Restorer, Picture- A video-cassette-player head-cleaning tape.

Results, Football Extra litter, broken shop windows, improved off-licence sales.

Retention, Water See Hosepipe Ban.

Retirement, Early Option now available to school-leavers.

Retraction The official withdrawal of harmful allegations which merely serves to make everyone believe that they were true.

Rev. Abbreviation indicating a reverend in the Church of England. See also 'Ms'.

Reversal of fortune Enutrof.

Review copy Pre-publication volume sold, unread, to secondhand bookshops by journalists for beer-money.

Review, Pay See 'Cut, Wages'.

Revised edition Book with less mistakes than its original printing.

Revised estimate Building trade term. An increased estimate.

Revision Listening to pop music with an open text-book in the room.

Revival, Theatrical The ham-acted on-field recovery of a footballer shamming a foul.

Revolution How any minor and often pointless modification of a product is described by advertisers. e.g. 'The chewable indigestion tablet – a revolution in the treatment of peptic distress symptoms!'

Revolutionary design Use of the word 'revolutionary' as a synonym for 1. Uncomfortable. 2. Ugly.

Rex Name given to dogs.

Rhyming slang Cockney verse-dialect term for a local group of villains i.e. 'Rhyming slang' = 'East End Gang'.

Rich pickings The financial reward for playing guitar for Genesis, the Rolling Stones, Dire Straits, etc.

Riddle of the Sands The allure of Clacton.

Right away! Tomorrow.

Rights, Human Lager, Nike trainers, and satellite TV.

Rip Van Winkle Pioneering M.E. sufferer.

Road sense 1. Avoiding motorways. 2. Not owning a car.

Robbery, Daylight Result of turning clocks backwards in winter.

Robust Cliché beloved of wine critics. The opposite of 'soft'.

Roll-on, roll-off 1. Modern ferries. 2. Modern sex.

Rolling Stones Rare example of group of old people for whom the young have respect and admiration.

Romantic movement See 'Pelvic Thrust'.

Rostrum camera Ken Morse.

Rotation, Crop The turning of market stall produce so that bad parts are hidden from customers.

Rotten Only member of Sex Pistols known to oldies.

Roundabout, Magic A rare traffic roundabout with genuinely helpful exit-signs.

Rucksack The burden of youth.

Rug-rats 1. American slang for babies. 2. Major rodent pest worry for Elton John and others.

Rule of thumb That the thumb shall appear in the foreground of all holiday photos.

Rustic charm A horseshoe.

S

Saboteurs, Hunt What frustrated fox-hunters are forced to do.

Sachet French word used to give false dignity to irritating paper portions of artificial sweetener.

Sacrament, Holy Religious precursor of the burger-bar concept: a fast moving stream of people served nutritionally-inadequate items by a person in ridiculous uniform.

Sacred Cows Farmers' view of any cattle qualifying for heavy EU subsidy.

Sacrifice, Great Those parents who forego buying a Tuscan holiday home or a third car to pay the children's school fees are said – by themselves only – to have made a great sacrifice.

Sacrosanct Hollow claim made by backbench Tories about any aspect of British life soon to be ruined or destroyed by either commercial greed or EU legislation e.g. 'The British Sunday/sausage/parliamentary system, etc. is sacrosanct.'

Saddlebag Scurrilous nickname for the Princess Royal.

Saint Michael Patron saint of quality underwear.

Sake of the Children. For the 1. Reason given by ill-matched partners for continuing to stay together. 2. Reason given by ill-matched partners for choosing to separate.

Salad days The time between the date of purchase and the 'Use By' date on M & S ready-to-eat salad selections.

Salary 1. The money given to employees in return for work. 2. The greater amount given to company chairmen and directors in return for keeping down 1.

Sale of Goods Act Extra dull act removed from final draft of Arthur Miller's 'Death of a Salesman'.

Sales, January Sales so-called because they begin on December 26th.

Sales-resistance 1. Poverty. 2. Death.

Salmonella An increasingly common food additive.

Salt, With a pinch of How most dietary health scares should be taken.

Sample, Free The provision of

urine, at no cost to the householder, by drunks who come into your garden at night.

Sampler Nowadays, a computer allowing contemporary 'musicians' to lift snatches of noise from other people's records. Formerly, a framed example of needlework bearing some Biblical text, such as 'Thou shall not steal'.

Sanctions 1. Trade embargo used by Western governments to restrict the sale of certain goods and weapons to out-of-line countries, thereby handily forcing up the price of those outlawed goods and weapons that they continue to supply covertly. 2. Delaying tactics used by politicians to buy more time for war preparations.

Sanskrit The language of the earliest Barbara Cartland novels.

Sapling Tree bent in half by vandals.

Sarcasm The lowest form of wit i.e. that used by policemen and magistrates.

Sardine The world's wealthiest fish – all of its relatives being in oil.

Satchel Child's stout leather school-case with pockets for video games, cigarettes, solvent products, aerosols, and lunchtime-burger money.

Satisfaction guaranteed or your money back Sign notable for its absence from British railway booking-halls.

Satisfactory condition Curious phrase used by doctors to describe the state of any attack or accident victim who, despite horrific injuries, is now asleep in a hospital bed.

Saturn Planet with pioneering ring-road system.

Sauce for the goose, Sauce for the gander Tomato ketchup, the universal condiment.

Sausage, Not a Brussels bombshell ruling on the good old British banger.

Save the whale! Cry heard at wildlife conservation rallies.

Save the whale 'til last! Cry heard in Japanese sushi restaurants.

Save face Command given by Michael Jackson to crack squad of cosmetic surgeons.

Saviour A person who puts money into a failing play or business.

Sawn-off shotgun Only known method for getting money out of banks without having to provide excessive personal details and at a favourable rate of interest.

Say Di, Never Instruction to all new staff in Prince of Wales' Highgrove hideaway.

Scaffolding Intricate metal bower erected by building-workers for the purpose of sexual display.
Scaling down Euphemism for job-shedding, or cuts to benefits and services.
Scam See 'Insurance' – Car, Health, National, etc.
Scampi Any unidentifiable chunk of white fish-matter to which a red stripe has been added using food dye is described on pub menus as scampi.
Scant regard The deep respect shown by the young towards the old.
Scape-goat See 'World recession', 'Brussels', 'Lady Thatcher', 'Labour Government, The Last', etc. Also 'The Pill', 'Television', 'The Sixties', 'School-teachers' and the 'CIA'.
Scarecrow Teenage fashion icon.
Scatter-cushion Self-serving description of any cushion a person cannot be bothered to replace on a sofa.
Scenario Theatrical term used to make life's banalities sound more dramatic e.g. 'What's the scenario vis a vis getting the car serviced/picking up your mother/shopping on Saturday,' etc.
Scenery Any range of hills visible from a road.
Schadenfreude Taking delight in others' misery i.e. the key to *EastEnders* popularity.
Schizophrenia Mental illness in which the poor sufferer hears voices telling him he is too expensive to care for and would be better off walking the streets.
Schooldays The unhappiest days of a teacher's life.
Science fiction Any nuclear industry report claiming atomic power is safe, efficient, and cheap to produce.
Scion Word encountered only in newspapers, and then applied only to the children of the upper classes.
Scone of Stone Scone sold by Inter City catering.
Scoop 1. A tabloid newspaper exclusive. 2. A device for picking up dog-dirt.

Scottish National Party Devolutionist group whose most famous supporter is Sean Connery – who lives in Spain.

Scratch 'n' sniff What the hyperallergic do all year round.

Screen, Silver The cinema screen – described as 'silver' as its stars so rapidly tarnish.

Sculpture, Modern Nowadays, any haphazard pile of household waste not actually awaiting collection by the bin-men.

Sea-change Money given for deckchairs at Blackpool.

Season ticket Rail commuter's necessity, popular with masochists.

Seasons, The Nature's poor attempt to mimic the fashion industry. She remains, rather pathetically, up to six months behind.

Seasons, Four 1. A singing group. 2. A type of pizza. 3. A tune by Nigel Kennedy.

Second-hand car salesman Profession that has never recovered from unfair association with Richard Nixon.

Sedentary occupation British workman's view of road-mending.

Self-defence The only circumstance in which it is thought that Hugh Grant or Roger Moore might be prompted to act.

Sell-by date Mark carried by various foods, hospitals, State railway companies, etc.

Seminal work Male prostitution.

Sensory deprivation unit An off-licence or public house.

Sensual Media cliché for any activity – aside from sex – that is performed by naked people. Thus, a video featuring a naked couple redecorating would be called 'The Art of Sensual Wallpapering', nude book-keeping – 'Sensual Accountancy', and so on. Displays of sexual intercourse, no matter how unappealing, are always described as 'erotic'.

Sentence, Long A rare find in the new, brittle journalism.

Sentry-duty Posing for photos next to US and Japanese tourists.

Sequel Any American movie which is not a remake. There are no sequels to British films as the concept implies that some previous film made money

Serenade, Donkey The self-congratulatory sing-song at the end of party conferences.

Service, Active Phenomenon rare in British restaurants.

Service, Civil Not to be expected

from railway platform staff.

Service, Poor The work of Crisis, Shelter, and the Save the Children Fund.

Set aside EU money reserved by farmers to build extensions onto their farmhouses.

Seventy mph A motorway speed limit. The upper limit is not specified.

Sex An advertising technique.

Sex-kitten Newspaper cliché attached to any schoolgirl whose parents allow her to be photographed wearing lipstick in a nightclub.

Shades of Night Sunglasses worn by nightclub poseurs.

Shah The late Terry Thomas's view of any proven incompetent e.g. 'You're a shah. An absolute shah'.

Shake up Business euphemism for job-losses.

Shaken, Badly Any champagne bottle handed to some fool sportsman.

Shakes, No Great Sad burger-chain truism.

Shape, In Good Assessment always qualified by the unspoken codicil '. . . . for his/her age'.

Share, Fair Equity held in Alton Towers.

Shatter one's illusions Heave a brick at the telly.

Shaver, Electric Ingenious device for removing all facial hairs but for one or two, which then grow to inordinate length.

She-wolf Nurtured Romulus and Remus.

She-woolf Nurtured Hogarth Press.

Sheaf A cockney condom.

Sheep, Acting Like The duty of Ambridge extras.

Sheikh Arabian aristocracy's gift to low comedy, as in Sheikhs Al-egg, N'Vac, Ratel En-rol, etc. See also Lords Elpus, Sprayer, and Luffer-Ducke.

Shelter, Bus Simple roadside shelter erected to keep the rain off vandals while they get on with their important work.

Shipwreck The UK boat-building industry.

Shock treatment Film treatment of novel that hasn't had extra sex and violence added.

Shoehorn See 'Foot-fetishism'.

Shook Up, All Postal-workers' rock‘n‘ roll favourite.

Shredded Wheat Processed breakfast product whose advertising seems to suggest that it is actually possible to eat more than one of the loathsome things

Shrine Any historic national sporting venue.

Shrug Resounding government response to its proven incompetence and dishonour.

Shut-down Any down over which the army do manoeuvres.

Sifting the Evidence When the police are thoroughly stumped they say they are sifting the evidence.

Similar Not the same as 'the same as', but similar.

Similarity to any living person is coincidental Principle underlying passport photographs.

Sink, Chained to the Kitchen What only the plug is nowadays.

Skilled Labour Result of regular attendance at ante-natal classes.

Skin and bone, Naught but See 'Sausagemeat'.

Skirl Word specially invented to describe the peculiar horror of bagpipes.

Sleepy, You Are Feeling Scurrilous accusation levelled at Snow White.

Sleeve The modern built-in handkerchief.

Sloth A notoriously slow creature. See also 'Daytime TV presenter'.

Smart Euphemism for stupid, as in smart weapon, smart drug, 'smart dress required', etc.

Smells, Bells and 1. High Church practices. 2. Whisky-drinking vagrants.

Smile, and the world smiles with you Now amended to 'Smile, and the world will think you're a bit odd in the head'.

Snap judgement The dispiriting self-assessment of one's holiday photos.

Snip at only £99 Private clinic's special offer of cut-price vasectomy.

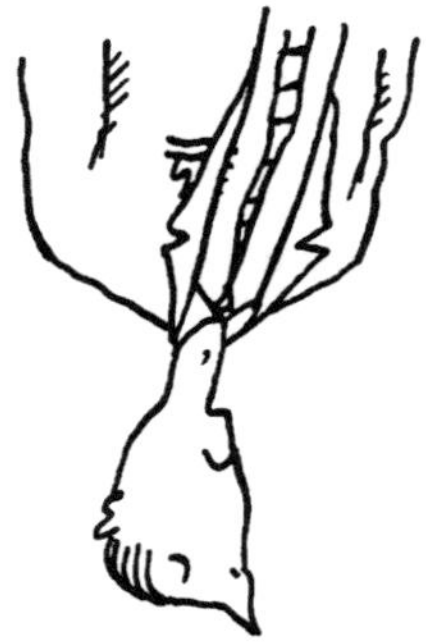

Snobbery, Inverted Snobbery

Snookered Put in a position without solution e.g. with nothing left to watch on TV but hours of dull potting from Sheffield.
Snoopy Long-lived non-smoking beagle.
Sober as a judge Drunk, but in a slumped, sitting position.
Social standing Also known as queuing.
Socialism Seemingly unworkable system in which the means of production, distribution and exchange are owned by the nation, as opposed to Capitalism, in which they are owned by the Americans, Germans, and Japanese.
Society, High The upper class demi-monde, with its prodigious use of stimulants.
Soft Word meaning 'not quite as bad as it could be', as in soft drugs, soft porn, soft sentence, soft furnishings, etc.
Software That part of a computer system that is easier to shoplift.
Soil, Top Soil bought from Harrod's.
Sold down the river The original residents of Docklands.
Soldier See 'Our boys'.
Solemn occasion TV sitcom watching.
Soliloquy Shakespearian forerunner of cabbies' conversation.
Solo Opportunity created by jazz musicians for audiences to catch up on conversation.
Sorbet 'Slush Puppy' for grown-ups.
Sorry Word absent from vocabulary of public transport employees.
Soufflé Critics' kind euphemism for any trite show in which one of their friends is appearing.
Soundbite Thought by media commentators to be a pernicious attempt to reduce the statements of politicians to a few catchy slogans – but with the positive benefit of drastically reducing the amount of rot we thus get to hear from them.
Space Race The fierce battle between motorists to find somewhere to park the car.
Sparrow Bird whose conviction for the murder of Cock Robin was largely based on confessional evidence.
Spate The collective noun for burglaries.
Speak of the Devil What the Anglican church no longer does.
Spelling bee Three-letter task which would tax quite a number of 11 year olds.
Splinter group The Carpenters.
Spoilsport What Sky and ITV do

with their excessive ad-breaks.

Sport of Kings Adultery.

Sprint, It's a Marathon, Not A Wrong on both counts. It's now a 'Snickers'.

Square-leg 1. Cricket position. 2. Picasso speciality.

Stamp One place where you will still find a flattering image of a member of the Royal family.

Stations of the Cross King's and Charing.

Statistics The triumph of mathematics over political debate.

Stealth bomber Military aeroplane so advanced that it only shows up noticeably on USA defence bills.

Stethoscope Device used by GPs when they choose to actually listen to their patients.

Still-life A traffic-jam.

Stools Between Two Where it is hoped the foot will fall on heavily dog-fouled pavements.

Strapped for cash Service available to masochists from prostitutes.

Strides, Making Great What Australian tailors claim to be doing.

Stubble-burning Consequence of cheap aftershave.

Subtle blend Every foul-tasting new addition to the available range of liqueurs is described by the marketing men as a 'subtle blend' of something or other.

Succeed, If at first you don't . . . You'll end up owing the banks a fortune.

Sugar The healthy alternative to artificial sweeteners.

Suicide, Political Remaining principled.

Summing up Period at end of court case when lawyers total up their bills.

Supermarket A small hypermarket.

Surface tension Result of face-lift.

Surgical bombing Military euphemism for bombing likely to result in victims requiring surgery.

Sweat, and Tears, Blood Easily removed with biological powders.

T

T-shirt Shirt without sleeves, collar, or taste.
Table Discussion, Round Dull hippy debate overheard at Glastonbury Festival camp-site.
Tablecloth A wipe-clean plastic sheet with or without cigarette burns.
Table-talk Frustrating 'Antiques Roadshow' chat prior to the expert's revelation of an item's likely worth.
Taboo, The Last Any taboo prior to the next to be broken is described as the last.
Tabs On, Keep Option available to label-conscious jeans-wearers.
Tacit support Support always claimed by those without support. See 'Liberal Democrats'.
Taciturn Cliché used to describe any 'super-star' who simply refuses to answer the prurient, immodest, or just plain stupid questions of journalists.
Tadpole Ageist term for a pre-adult frog.
Tailor's dummy Any idiot catwalk mannequin.
Tails, Slugs and Snails and Puppy-dogs' Contents labelling now required by law on every male human juvenile.
Take-away food Ploy used by waiters trying to chivvy end-of-evening diners.
Take credit To steal Access cards.
Take place How banks and building societies deal with mortgage defaulters.
Taken out of context 1. Invariably, any single word taken from a newspaper review and used to promote a West End drama or movie. The word will always have three dots either side e.g. '. . . unstoppable . . .' 2. The Englishman abroad.
Take it to heart What the blood stream does with cholesterol.
Taken to task See 'commuting'.
Taking stock The first stage in recovery from hunger-strike.
Tale Ending, Fairy Being chopped to pieces by a woodman.

Talk of the town What rich people do in the country at weekends.
Talk is cheap Assertion refuted by lawyers and mobile telephone companies.
Talks about talks The positive outcome of talks about talks about talks.
Tamper-proof seal Amphibious mammal safe from perverts.
Tandem A welcome attempt to halve the number of noisy, polluting bicycles to be found on roads today.
Tangled web we weave, O what a Poetic claim made in hair transplant clinic advertisement.
Tanker, Oil An accident waiting to happen.
Tap, Phone An example of democracy in action i.e. the government listening to the people.
Tar and feathers Result of over-microwaving poultry.
Tarbrush, A touch of the Phrase implying racialist concern about ancestry.
Tarbuck, A touch of the Phrase implying understandable concern about ancestry.
Target, Bang on What very few of the West's so-called 'smart' bombs actually managed to do in the Gulf.
Target, Moving 1. The road-crossing pedestrian. 2. Trackside vandals' view of railway train.
Taste, Bad The jokes about atrocities rather than those atrocities themselves, oddly.
Taste, Good One's own taste reflected in others.
Tattoo, Military A knife dripping blood, 'Mum', Belfast 1971–73, etc.
Tax, Liable to Euphemism for 'alive'.
Taxidermy The last chance Britain has of preserving its wildlife.
Teledu The stinking badger of Java. (Not a joke, but an interesting item of trivia.)
Television licence The liberty that is taken by certain broadcasters with respect to truth and decency.
Tell, William Parent whose child would today be removed into care.
That Old Black Magic Reduced to 99p a box for quick sale.
That's another fine mess Phrase now associated with modern art criticism.
Therapy, Occupational Treatment denied at least two million unemployed.
Thick and thin How most pop-stars prefer their girlfriends.
Thirteen Unlucky for 1. Some. 2. Parents with children of this age.

Three blind mice Politically-incorrect nursery rhyme. Now amended to 'Three visually-impaired but still valid members of the rodent community'.
Throne, The power behind the The British tourism and souvenir industries.
Throw-away society What Mrs Thatcher seemed rather eager to do.
Tick, Sheep Mark made by farmer on EU Lamb Subsidy Form.
Ticker, Dodgy Watch sold from suitcase in Regent Street.
Tidal wave 1. Standard media description for any small number of letters received in protest about something. 2. Last gesture of end-it-all *Mirror* publisher.
Tidiness Obvious sign of some neurotic compulsive disorder.
Tie The one item of male clothing sold at railway stations.
Tie the knot Figure of speech doomed by the spreading use of Velcro.
Tie me kangaroo down, sport Seminal Rolf Harris number abhorred by animal rightists for continuing to associate animal cruelty with 'sport'.
Tied up at the moment, He's all Literal truth often spoken unwittingly by many an MP's secretary.
Tight, Sit Best advice for avoiding bruising when travelling on awful 'Hoppa' buses.
Tight security 1. Any level of security yet to be exposed as a sham is described as tight. 2. Drunken building guards.
Tiles, A night on the A charity Scrabble marathon.
Time-gentlemen, please Polite request made at Dr Who convention.
Time, Doing How Stephen Hawking describes his work at parties.
Time frame Repulsive pseudo-science buzzword used by morons who think that saying 'What timeframe are we talking about?' is so much more efficient and go-getting than 'How long will it take?'
Time-honoured Cliché used of any pointless ritual with nothing to commend it other than for how long it has been performed.
Timetable, Railway A triumph of hope over experience.
Timid Word used to describe any wild creature which refuses to make an idiot of itself in return for scraps of stale bread.

Tinderbox How the media describe all those small disturbed nations which they have not otherwise described as 'powderkegs'.
Tinned Word meaning 'not frozen'.
Tip A payment made in return for 1. Good service. 2. Avoiding a scene. 3. Getting council workers to do what they're paid for.
Tireless Synonymous with ineffectual or monomaniacal, as in 'This tireless campaigner . . . ' etc.
Tissue of lies See 'Government white paper'.
Tit-head Rupert Murdoch.
T-junction Now obsolete. See 'mini-roundabout'.
To be or not to be Shakespearian dilemma.
Toby or not Toby Middle-class christening dilemma.
Toff The tabloid headline writers' space-saving aristocrat.
Toilet-water The nature of the sea close by many a British resort.
Tomato A ketchup flavour.
Tone The Essex Anthony.
Tone poem Standard excuse for any dull piece of music without recognisable tune or interest.
Tonight Mis-spelling of 'tonite'.
Tooth and nail Low quality sausage meat components.
Toothbrush Device for promoting tooth-loss through accelerated gum erosion.
Top, Big Obvious career advantage for would-be page 3 models.
Topicality Excuse used by unfunny satirists.
Top secret Legend stamped on government documents to ensure their speedy return from phone-boxes, cafes, bus-shelters, etc.
Torrid Word inevitably used to describe any TV sex scene where the viewer feels a need to turn the volume down.

Torso The largest section of the human body that will fit comfortably into a bin-liner.
Toss, Winning the A British sporting victory.
Tot The tabloid headline writers' space-saving 'infant'.
Touchtone Phone allowing customers to play pretty tunes as they dial wrong numbers.
Tour-de-force Standard critics'

cliché for any play in which one actor singlehandedly harangues and bores an audience for over two hours.

Tourist 1. A despised foreign visitor. 2. A despised English cricketer.

Tournament, Royal The battle between the Windsors and their former spouses.

Towel, Roller Washroom 'Test-Your-Strength' machine.

Tower, Sent to the Seemingly every overseas visitor with access to a nylon rucksack.

Toxic, Non- Safety claim made, intriguingly, for pencil crayons rather than foodstuffs.

Toy-boy Youth with unusual interest in the elderly.

Trace Element Sharon ('Shaz') Element's sister.

Track record Steam enthusiast's favourite listening.

Trade Union 1. A coalition of working people. 2. A coalition of formerly working people.

Trade wind What Gazza and his chums love to do after a particularly active curry.

Trading places Wall Street, the Stock Exchange, the Bourse, etc.

Traditional Term used to describe any extinct folk-practice recently revived to aid the sale of brown bread, beer, or country cottage holidays.

Traffic, Heavy Those vehicles returning from cross-Channel duty-free shopping trips.

Trailer A cinema advertisement used to imply, spuriously, that the film being promoted contains other entertaining moments besides those used to make the trailer.

Train-spotting Bound to get much harder after further rail privatisation.

Transcendental meditation Pseudo-religious exercise in which people focus their minds on matters beyond their range of experience e.g. reality, commonsense, healthy scepticism, etc.

Transistor radio Radio so small and, hence, so portable, that it can annoy people anywhere in the world.

Transit Type of van stolen by

thieves and terrorists.

Transmission The spread of 1. Diseases. 2. Television programmes.

Transports of delight What the tube and train system used to be.

Trappist About the only religious extremist you won't hear on a radio phone-in.

Tray Device for carrying large quantities of lager outside the human body.

Tree A cable TV obstruction.

Trespass No doubt by sheer coincidence, a perfect rhyme of 'Press Pass'.

Trial run The on-foot escape of prisoners from custody.

Triangle, Bermuda Area notorious for the eery disappearance of whole aircraft, not just their passengers' luggage.

Tribute, Moving Praise given to removal men for not breaking all the china.

Tricks Campaign, Dirty The growing movement to promote pornographic conjuring.

Triton 1. A brand of shower-bath. 2. What Cockneys ask to do in clothes-shops.

Tropical Advertisers' pathetic slant on any product that contains coconut.

Trouble in store Dire consequence of trying to smuggle nine items through the 'Eight or fewer' queue.

Trowel, Lay it on with a What Michael Jackson must do.

True-love gave to me, My Plaint heard in VD clinics all year round.

Trump In Britain, a vulgar flatus. In the States, a vulgar tycoon.

Trustees The collective noun for people who sell Britain's heritage to foreigners.

Truth, The A legal impediment.

Turkish delight Any Greek set-back.

Turn on, tune in, drop out 1960s bead-time radicals' rubric.

Turn on, tune in, drop off Over 60s bedtime radio ritual.

Turn up for the books What VAT inspectors from the Customs & Excise do on a regular basis.

Twin town Foreign town chosen by councillors as expenses-paid holiday destination.

Two's Company . . . Three's an unauthorised gathering. (Old Libyan proverb).

Typographical error See 'Economic recovery'.

Tzigane Hungarian gypsy popular with Scrabble fans.

U

UB40 1. The unlucky small businessman's business card.
2. Phonetic Mummerset birthday greeting, as in 'O, R, U B 40, B U? O, R,' etc.

Udder An Americanism, as in 'udder disaster', 'udderly disgustin', etc.

Ugly duckling Despite fiction and the hopes of Chelsea Clinton, an ugly duck precursor.

Ulcer That gut-feeling most big businessmen have.

Ultimate Salesmen's euphemism for 'the most pointlessly expensive model currently available' e.g. 'This, sir, is the ultimate in in-car entertainment'.

Ultra Prefix meaning 'bonkers', as in Ultra-Right Wing, Ultra-Left, etc.

Ultrasonic Level of sound audible only to dogs and those who love complaining to hotel-managers.

Ululation A loud howling.
And, curiously, a perfect anagram of Lulu-ation.

Umbilical cord Mother Nature's very own child safety rein.

Umbilical cords Stretch-fabric trousers worn by expectant mothers.

Umbrage Spiritual home of disaffected Archers fans.

Umpire, Tennis An official so unpopular that he is placed on a high chair out of reach of enraged players.

Umpteenth Time, The That occasion on which teenagers and public servants finally consent to do what you've been asking of them.

Un- Indicates reversal or negation.

U.N. See above.

Unacceptable, Wholly Acceptable, eventually.

Un-American activities Whispering, wearing caps correctly, receiving medical care when poor, allowing cultural treasures to stay in Europe, pronouncing 'Leicester' properly, making fun of successful people, drinking beer that tastes of something, not believing Benny Hill a genius, etc.

Unashamed See 'Mellor'.

Unawares, Caught Most venereal diseases.

Unbeknownst Word developed by the Elizabethans for later use by Jeremy Beadle.

Uncalled for About ten per cent of

all completed dry-cleaning.

Uncertainty 1. A particle physicists' principle. 2. A government economic strategy.

Uncharitable act Any act that refuses to appear for free on 'Comic Relief' night.

Unchecked, Allowed To Go The sad, forgotten souls in many a poorly-run old peoples' home.

Uncivilised country Defined now as any country in which the opening of a new McDonald's is still considered an example of progress.

Uncle Tom's Cabin Now expanded as 'Uncle Tom's Stay-A-While Cabin Complex' and 'Cotton Pickers™ Soul-Food Restaurant'.

Unclean! Unclean! A traditional British beach-cry.

Uncommonly good Modern tautology. Anything good nowadays is, by definition, uncommon.

Unconditional love 1. That shown by dogs for people. 2. Replaced at the behest of lawyers by the pre-nuptial agreement.

Unconditional surrender An Iraqi moral victory.

Uncontrollable urges Those urges which the sufferer chooses not to control.

Unconventional Word used to make polite allowance for the behaviour of any person who is bonkers but rich or influential. Everyone else is just a loony.

Uncooperative Police assessment of any witness with a penchant for falling down stairs.

Uncut version How pretentious, 'auteur theory' bakers like to refer to their yet-to-be-sliced loaves.

Underacting A base accusation to level at Donald Sinden.

Undercover, Working See 'Blanket, Electric'.

Undergrad Now reverted to its former name of St Underberg.
Undergraduate humour See 'Radio humour, three years later'.
Underground movement A violent sideways jerking with long pauses in between.
Underlay The flooring about which Speedy Gonzales – The Fastest Mouse In Mexico – is always shouting. ('Underlay! Underlay! Arriba! Arriba!).
Underpass Eloquent proof that the only real thing for which a road will actually be diverted at great expense is another road.
Underwater sequences Those parts in spy films where you no longer know who is who – nor care.
Underworld The new crime-based theme-park planned for London's East End.
Undesirable element Plutonium.
Undiscovered Travel brochure euphemism for that area of the globe that the trade has decided to ruin next.
Undress, State of California, if 'Baywatch' is anything to go by.
Unemployment benefit No longer having to commute.
Unerring French for an unsmoked kipper.
Unexpected pleasure Any pleasure afforded by daytime TV.
Unfurnished Recently burgled.
Unique selling point The marketing men's name for a gimmick.
Unisex What every fresh undergraduate thinks they are going to get lots of.
Unit, Retail A shop, as in 'Ye Olde Curiosity Retail Unit', etc.
University challenge Getting Britons to study science subjects.
University of Life Academic institution with deplorably low entrance requirements.
Unnatural act Widely-held impression of The Krankies.
Unnecessary suffering See 'Eurovision Song Contest'.
Unoccupied premises Those new London offices whose doorways afford such valuable shelter to the homeless.
Unparliamentary language Swearing, rather than the telling of bare-faced lies.
Unpopular Synonym for 1. French. 2. Healthy. 3. British, rather than American. 4. Sensible. 5. Educational.
Unprincipled Elected.
Unprofessional conduct Working for free.

Unqualified success TV funster Paul Merton.
Unrest TV news cliché. The throwing of stones in foreign town centres.
Unscripted Any simple question which puts a politician off his stride.
Unskilled labour See 'school-leaver'.
Unspoilt countryside Obviously poor building land.
Unstuck, Come What dental crowns do on holidays.
Unswerving loyalty Loyalty yet to be made a better offer.
Untimely death Any death during your GP's favourite TV programme.
Unvarnished Truth, The Known in trendy north London as 'The Stripped Pine Truth'.
Up, Up, and Away First line of chorus of 'Beautiful Balloon' song.
Up, Up, and Aweh Firm of Nigerian lawyers.
Urinal See 'phone-box'.
Useful life What many civil servants could yet be capable of leading.
User-friendly Odd term implying that some new machines are not actually designed with purchasers in mind.
Utter nonsense What astrologers, crystal-therapists, and aura-readers do.

V

Vacant, Situations Those situations encountered in the average TV sit-com.

Vacuum, Nature abhors a Scientific rule-of-thumb now updated to read, 'Nature and those people in the flat below abhor a vacuum'.

Vagabond Special government index-linked investment unit available to tramps, the homeless, and down-and-outs.
Vague recollection Perfect recollection obscured merely by the fear of blame.
Valet of Death Concept regularly encountered in bad country house murder stories i.e. the butler did it.
Valiant effort The approved commentators' cliché for any British sporting failure.
Valley, Silicon Californian region devoted to electronics.
Valley, Silly Cone British motorway cutting undergoing roadworks.
Valuable 1. Any item of your property for which some thief might conceivably get a fiver down the pub. 2. Every last scrap of Britain's heritage and countryside under threat from greedy people.
Value, Added Contemptible concept used to inflate the cost of an item beyond its worth, and make it liable to VAT. Thus, a piece of raw coal may be worth less than 1p. Tied with ribbon and glued to a card saying, 'A Present from t'Pits', it has added value and sells for £1.99, with the government getting 30p.
Value Added Tax The tax that should be levied on those making the sort of souvenir described above.
Valued customer How banks in junk mail-shots refer to all customers whom they wish to inveigle into some expensive new credit scheme.
Van Trade vehicle used to transport labourers between dole offices.
Vandal One who wilfully damages property or land without a contract from the government.
Vanishing point That point immediately after handing over a large amount of money to a cowboy company when they suddenly disappear forever from their premises.
Vanity case Lawsuit brought against cosmetic surgeons for alleged malpractice.
Various authors Suspicion now harboured about all police-extracted confessions.
Veal Meat from cows denied the chance to grow up and develop BSE.
Vector A broad Scots winner.
Velveteen A difficult age for velvet.
Vending-machine 1. A punchbag placed on platforms for the benefit of tube and rail passengers. 2. A burger-bar employee.
Veneer Coating applied to valuable

chipboard to protect it from harm.

Venerable Polite euphemism for 'successful but past it'.

Venetian blind? How do you make a Old joke whose punchline is now updated to 'Expose him to dog-dirt infected with toxacara worms'.

Ventilator Piece of hospital equipment available to any smoker with 500,000 coupons.

Ventriloquism What all Rupert Murdoch's editors keep having to deny that they practice.

Venture, This exciting new The past tense of 'this spectacular business failure'.

Verbal warning Warning that ought to be made to sensitive viewers before Loyd Grossman speaks on television.

Verdict, Open Peter Alliss's annual retrospective view.

Vermin Category into which nearly all the most popular cartoon animals fall.

Verse, Free Use of the word 'free' as a synonym for 'rubbish'. See also free jazz, free gift, free flights offer, etc.

Versus Legal term. A prefix to the words 'Private Eye'.

Vertigo Classic Hitchcock film inspiring much zany video-shop humour e.g. Customer: 'Do you have Vertigo?' Assistant: 'No, I live above the premises!'.

Veto The least co-operative of the Sackville-Wests.

Vexed What German Barbour jackets are.

Via The cockneys' favourite Sackville-West.

Vibrations, Good How a dwindling number of obstetricians now view ultrasound.

Vic, The Old 1. Victor Sylvester. 2. Victor Meldrew. 3. Vic Damone. 4. Vapour rub.

Vic, The Young 1. Vic Reeves. 2. Vikram Seth.

Vicar 1. A Church of England minister. 2. A character often encountered in farce (see 1).

Vice Squad, The A humorously named Soho joinery firm.

Vicious circle 1. The M25. 2. The former associates of 'Sex Pistol' Sid.

Victim Support See 'crutches'.

Victoria, Queen Pub featured in *EastEnders.*

Victorian values 1. An outmoded belief in God, the family, side-whiskers, child labour, and cholera. 2. Now appreciated only by those in the antiques trade.

Video nasties What cameras in banks and shopping centres are discreetly placed there to do.

Video-recorder 1. Useful device affording the operator the supreme convenience of choosing for themselves exactly when to not quite get round to watching all the programmes they have taped. (Will also record up to 8 hours of the wrong channel at the touch of a button.) 2. The one challenge life still holds for the over-sixties.

Vigour Ian Paisley's 'vicar'.

Village Hampstead's greatest deception. In London the term means essentially any small area whose street name-plates still differ from the standard council issue. To estate agents it may consist of no more than a single street with an all-night store at one end.

Village idiot Any indigenous yokel who sells the family cottage too low and too soon.

Vineyard A large, boring and ugly field on the Continent, as opposed to one in Britain.

Vintage Euphemism for 'rubbish, but old rubbish', and used as a poor excuse for re-running bad films and sit-coms on TV e.g. 'Vintage comedy now on BBC1 as the staff of Grace Brothers ask 'Are You Being . . . ?' etc.

Violins, Sex and Content of film about Antonio Vivaldi.

VIP lounge Place where dull celebrities and businessmen pay more to pass the same amount of time waiting in the same airport for the same plane as poor people.

Virgin territory Territory fiercely contested by the BBC and British Airways.

Virginia creeper An over-ingratiating Heritage Department civil servant.

Virtual reality Cutting-edge computer science project in which companies are investing millions of dollars in a frenzied attempt to reproduce an effect which can currently be achieved by simply looking out of the window.

Virtue Gesundheit.

Visible consumption Formerly a sign of advanced tuberculosis, it now means buying things for your neighbours to covet.

Viviparous Bringing forth young alive, rather than laying eggs like Baroness Thatcher.

Vocation Defined as any badly paid job which someone has taken out of choice.

Vocational guidance Advising

your friends not to become teachers or nurses.

Volatile situation A peaceful situation plus television cameras.

Volume of traffic 'The Highway Code', HMSO, price 99p

Voluminous Standard cliché for any sizeable correspondence.

Voluntary contributions Contributions which one has to be asked to make.

Vomit An anagram of 'Vimto'.

Votes for Women What the more liberal Garrick club member does.

Vowels In Loyd Grossman's alphabet, those letters with stretchmarks.

Voyeur One who derives pleasure from watching i.e. not your average TV viewer.

W

Wacky Adjective meaning 'amusing to students only'.

Wage-slave Japanese term of endearment.

Wagon Great name for a trendy new soft-drink, as when friends ask if you want a lager, you can reply, 'No thanks, I'm on the Wagon'.

Wailing Wall A place of lamentation, and the religious precursor of the railway ticket-window.

Waist not, want not The anorexics' credo.

Wait for no man 1. What time and a tide, and mean bus-drivers do. 2. The only obvious merit of private healthcare.

Wake the dead, It's almost enough to The noise of any particularly raucous House of Lords debate.

Wake up England! Former 1930s anti-Nazi rallying cry. Now what car-alarms do every night.

Wales Former traditional name of the new Nipponese Business Park.

Wales, Prince of Title naturally given to that Royal who owns most of Cornwall.

Walk-on role What carpeting has in the homes of actors.

Walking distance, Within What the nearest pavement dog-turd always is.

Walks of life, People from different A Monty Python sketch.

Wall Street A place where jokes are made about the 'strength' of sterling.

Wall, Writing on the Private property. Keep out. These premises are patrolled by dogs, etc.

Walls of Jericho Short-lived biblical ice-cream company.

Wanted by the police More police, long-handled batons, stop and search, basically anything that makes them look more American.

Wanted man Like, peace, is, you know?

War, Cold Battle between office employees to claim the worst 'flu symptoms.

Ward, Private 1. A euphemistically-named urino-genital ward. 2. Soon to be promoted to Corporal Ward.

Warder What American health-bores choose instead of alcohol.

Warehouse A large storage space in which, well, we might have another one, but, you know, it could be two or three weeks until our next delivery. Have you tried our Watford branch?

Warm-blooded What scientists now believe Lord Tebbit may indeed be.

Warm personality Character trait noticed in ugly people.

Warmer! You're getting Children's thimble-hunting cry, now taken up by global ecologists.

Warning, Flood The gist of every right-wing MP's speech on immigration.

Warning, A Few Words of 'New', 'Improved'. 'Advanced', 'Tastier than ever', 'Alcohol-free', etc.

Warped mind M^{1}nd.

Warren 1. A place where rabbits breed. 2. Shirley Maclaine's oddly appropriately named brother.

Wartime From 0000 to 2400 hours, daily.

Wash and brush-up A bizarre and unseemly post-fox-hunting ritual.

Wash and go 1. An overhyped shampoo. 2. The landowners' plea to New Age travellers.

Wash your hands, Now 1. Sign always found in toilets next to a filthy roller-towel. 2. US foreign policy.

Washed down with Cliché used by those food writers who obviously wish to make eating and drinking sound like hosing out an elephant house.

Washed up What Robert Maxwell was, though his corpse, ironically, wasn't.

Washing your dirty linen in public A major embarrassment, as it thus reveals to the world that you can't afford a washing-machine.

Wasp An oddity of nature – a creature with a tiny waist, yet it spends all its time in cake-shops.

Waste disposal unit See 'Jobcentre'.

Waste, Lay Non-professional or non-ordained waste.

Waste of breath 1. Karaoke. 2. The harmonica.

Waste paper 1. Labour election leaflets in the south of England. 2. Tory election leaflets in Scotland. 3. All Ecology Party leaflets, ironically.

Wasteland The great new T. S. Eliot theme-park.

Wasting police time Protesting your innocence if young, black, or Irish.

Watch, Keep What terrified, tongue-tied victims tell muggers.

Watch what you're doing Now all too easily possible, thanks to the video camera.

Water A cheap, naturally-occurring form of Perrier.

Watered down Distressing result of the combination of a weak bladder and a duvet.

Waterlogged Result of domestic meter being fitted.

Waterloo BR station named prophetically after a common euphemism for a defeat.

Watershed TV term for 9pm. That time after which children must go to their rooms in order to keep watching the television.

Waves, It comes in Used toilet paper, rotting seaweed, disposable nappies, old condoms, tampons, etc.

Way, Pay One's See 'Privatised roads'.

Way to go home, Show me the *Cri de coeur* of M25 motorists.

W. C. Fields See 'dog-toilet'.

We are not amused 1. 19th

century Royal judgement. 2. 20th century judgement of Royal antics. 3. Common complaint of TV sit-com audiences.

We wish you a merry Christmas Seasonal refrain preluding doorstep 'money with menaces' demands.

Weak president Defined as any US leader who has to be bullied into sending troops abroad.

Weaker Sex, The Males, when it comes to child custody cases.

Weakness, Sign of The '£' sign.

Wealth creation See 'forgery'.

Wear and tear What the fan of distressed denim jeans does.

Wear down What geese do.

Wear, Evening See 'condom'.

Weary, World Term meaning 'sick of theme-parks'.

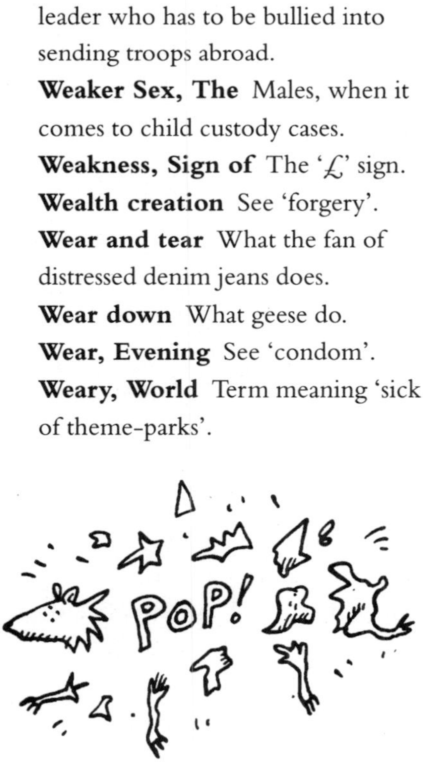

Weasel-word Pop.

Weather British synonym for rain, as in 'Just look at the weather . . . '

Weather balloon How one fondly hopes the Establishment on other planets explains our satellites to its people.

Weather-beaten What most British summer sporting fixtures are.

Weather pitch, All- The TV meteorologists' spiel.

Weather-girl An intellectual giant of early morning television.

Weatherman, TV A man who talks too quickly whilst pointing to a rapidly changing set of baffling electronic images – which we know he can't actually see – and then expects us to take him seriously. His career-goal is to be impersonated by a comedian.

Weather, Under the Some irritating little note saying 'Sponsored by Powergen' etc.

Weaver bird Strip-club MC's opening gambit. 'Weaver bird 'ere 'oos come all the way from Dagenham . . . ' etc.

Webber or not? 1. Dilemma facing discerning musical theatre lovers. 2. Potentially libellous speculation generating tens of thousands for lawyers.

Webbing Adenoidal marriage ceremony.

Wedding cake The major threat to Liz Taylor's diet plans.

Wedding ring See 'wife-swapping circle'.

Wedding souvenirs, Royal A cottage on the Gatcombe estate, an ugly house in Berkshire, half of Kensington Palace, a seventeen million pound lump sum, six grand-children from broken homes, etc.

Wedgey 1. US slang for buttock-strangling underpants. 2. UK slang for Anthony Wedgewood Benn.

Wedlock Type of lock easily undone nowadays.

Wee Frees Rigid Scots religious sect.

Wee freeze Likely in outside loos during winter.

Weed, The Dreaded According to age, either stinging nettles or tobacco.

Week Name given to any marketing exercise which lasts for up to seven days e.g. 'National Sausage Week.'

Weekend break A Sunday soccer league sporting injury.

Weekend, Dirty DIY on Saturday, gardening on Sunday.

Weekend, Long Any weekend spent in Milton Keynes.

Weight Machine, I Speak Your Machine known only to cartoonists.

Weighty matters Those individually trivial matters which go to make up each back-breaking edition of the *Sunday Times*.

Welcome to Wales What most English people would say the Welsh people are.

Well as can be expected, As Ill.

Well-trained What the subsequent Accident Inquiry showed that Jack and Jill patently were not. They were ordered to attend a compulsory Bucket Management course.

Wench Any female film extra in a bodice.

Westernize Round, not slitty, as Prince Philip would rush to explain.

Weston, Spaghetti Great name for a Somerset coastal resort pasta bar.

Wetland Heathite theme-park. (Only open three days a week.)

Wet nurse Health service worker unable to afford decent raincoat.

Whale oil Bad radio drama Irishism, as in, 'Whale oil be blowed!'

What you see is what you get (WYSIWYG) Rule which may be true in computing, but is certainly not in those fast-food restaurants where they have tempting pictures of your 'meal options' above the counter.

Wheel, The Potter's Innocent 1950s TV filler.

Wheel, Dennis Potter's A phallic column of wet clay, raised higher and higher to the accompaniment of an Al Bowlly record, intercut with scenes of Forest of Dean fornication.

When push comes to shove Rush hour on the Tube.

When the chips are down A computer malfunction.

Where angels fear to tread Area with high dog-ownership.

Where do you get your ideas? Tedious question which only writers and the insane get asked. The insane attempt to answer it.

While ye may, Gather ye rose-buds While the park-keeper's not looking.

Whispering grass Grass trying hard not to be overheard by Prince Charles.

Whistler's Mother Popular title for the Victorian painting more accurately known as 'That Miserable Old Bat In The Chair'.

White heat of technology See 'ceramic hob'.

Whole body scanner An exceedingly thorough building-site lecher.

W.I. A brazen band of blue-rinsed brigands who laugh in the face of the law with their EU-proscribed scone and jam-making activities.

Wicked stepmother Youth-speak for a superlative stepmother, as in, 'Hey, man! You gotta wicked stepmother!'

Wicket, Slow Wicket with the intelligence of the average England selector.

Wide berth, Give it a Ship-steward's insolent instruction re the booking of cabin for a cruise by the Duchess of York.

Wide of the Mark What sterling sadly is.

Widening scheme, Road Euphemism for what is more alarmingly a countryside-narrowing scheme.

Wider Still and Wider 1. 'Land of Hope and Glory' line loathed by those with fear of dentists. 2. Well-known firm of solicitors.

Wild child A wayward upper class teenager. Their behaviour is, however, merely a cry for attention – from the media.

Wildflowers Those plants that have to be dug up surreptitiously from woods rather than shoplifted from garden-centres.

Wildfowl Trust What duck-hunters gain before blasting their quarry from the water.

Wildlife Name given by townies to creatures killed by farmers.

Willing accomplice See 'Cabinet Minister'.

Wind blows, When the Faults in double-glazing become apparent.

Wind, Fire and Water, Earth The four elements of 1. Ancient Greece. 2. Household insurance.

Window of opportunity Burglar's slang for an open window.

Window-box Unnecessary packaging accompanying replacement window.

Windswept How the streets are kept clean in Britain's poorer boroughs.

Wine, British Blended foreign wine for which this gallant nation nobly takes the blame.

Wing Aircraft, Fixed Aeroplane whose faulty wing has now been repaired.

Wing, Left or Right How estranged Royal couples divide up shared residences.

Winged horse Horse grazed by pellet fired by vandal with air-rifle.

Winker Watson Famous 'Dandy Comic' schoolboy lucky never to have encountered the Reverend Spooner.

Winning that counts, It's not the . . . It's the fee for taking part. (Old English proverb.)

Wire, Copper An Interpol telegraph message.

Wire-tap Why not a tap? (Copyright Chico Marx, 1929).

Wisdom of the ancients Only possible explanation for how primitive men could site Stonehenge so that some 3000 years later it would be within walking distance of the main-road.

Wiretap.

Wisdom of the gods Cloth-capped comedian Norman as seen from the cheapest seats.

Wisdom teeth On average, the last teeth that Britons have filled.

Wish upon a star, When you 1. It turns out to be some fool man-made satellite. 2. You end up getting eaten by a whale.

Wishful thinking See 'England World Cup hopes'.

Wishing-well Bizarre public perception of every ugly shopping centre fountain.

Wisteria Benefit concert in aid of diseased climbing shrubs.

Wit Defined by TV as jokes made by people sitting down.

Wit, To See 'Barn owl'.

Witchcraft A broomstick.

Wive's Tale, Old Evidence given in divorce court.

Woad How Britons got blue in the face in the days before road-rage.

Wobbly, Throw a 1. To become suddenly angry. 2. Sumo-wrestling in a nutshell.

Woman, Fallen A bungee-jumping female.

Womb A short-stay child-care centre.

Women's issues *Hello!, Bella, Top Sante, OK* etc.

Women's movement Despite 25 years of feminism, still leeringly closely observed by building-site workers.

Women's problems 1. Traditionally, the Departments of Health, Education, and Social Security. 2. Men.

Wonder of the age What does John Gummer know that kept him in government for so long?

Wonderland, Alice in Masterpiece of fiction, rather like the TV soap 'Dallas' in that events turn out conveniently to have been 'all a dream'.

Woo, To See 'To wit'.

Wood Sprite Brand of lemonade drunk on forest picnic.

Woodpile Large sum of money saved by investing in tax-cushioned timber.

Woollen underwear See 'Seven year itch'.

Woolly-minded Gyles Brandreth, Noel Edmonds, and Richard Branson.

Word count See 'Lord Archer'.

Word on the streets, The No entry, Bus lane Look right, etc.

Words of wisdom 1. Buy our toothbrushes! 2. Mr Grimsdale! Mr Grimsdale! etc.

Work afoot, Dirty See 'Chiropody'.

Work cut out, Have one's The fate of writers faced with over-zealous sub-editors.

Work for idle hands, The devil finds More than Jobcentres do.

Work hard, play hard Bob Hoskins's acting technique.

Work it out, We can Defiant phrase used with respect to 1. Rocky relationships. 2. Video recorder operation.

Work, Whistle while you What faulty hearing-aids do.

Worker, Part-time Full-time worker who knows just what he or she can get away with.

Workers of the world, unite! You have nothing to lose but your pensions, overtime allocations, production bonuses, employee healthcare schemes, product purchasing discounts, creche facilities, jobs, self-respect, homes, etc.

Working from home See 'Televised Test cricket'.

World Term meaning 1. 'Foreign' or 'non-commercial', as in world cinema, world music, world peace, etc. 2. 'North American' or 'highly commercial', as in World Series, World Wrestling Federation, Disney World, etc.

World leaders Coca Cola, Disney, Nissan, Sony, etc.

World of Adventures, Chessington Grand name given to what is actually the more prosaic, 'Chessington, Small Surrey Suburb of Adventures'.

World of leather See 'Gay scene'.

World, Spirit A discount liquor-mart.

World without end 'Infinityland', the great new space-time continuum theme-park.

Worth hanging onto All passenger-rails in moving 'Hoppa' buses.

Wrapped up in his work Many a cabaret escapologist.

Wrecking crew The 1983 Thatcher government.

Wriggle out of it Standard procedure of extrication from tight-fitting Lycra garments.

Wrist-watch Watch kept by potential thief on Rolex Oyster wearer.

Writer's Block A posh set of flats in Hampstead.

Writing on the wall 'Please do not write on this wall'.

Wrong side of the law Facing the front of the law when the top of the stairs is behind you.

Wrongdoings See 'Fouled pavement'.

XYZ

X 1. The newspaper sign of the cross, as in 'What the XXXX is going on?' etc. 2. Roman numeral used to conceal the age of TV repeats. 3. An old film classification certificate, now roughly equivalent to today's 'PG'.

X-Files Dossiers kept by stalkers on former boyfriends of target.

XL Legend on label found inside most small shrunken T-shirts.

Xmas Popular festival, made to sound like a skin condition.

X-rays 1. How Salman Rushdie reads his post. 2. What 'Super-waif' modelling shots are often mistaken for.

XS That level to which tacky abbreviations are used nowadays.

Yacht 1. A 'Hello!' magazine photo-shoot prop. 2. Prize given to landlocked gameshow contestants.

Yam Popeyesque verb, as in 'I yam what I yam'.

Yamaha A type of loud motorbike or electronic organ. From the Japanese for 'irritating noise'.

Yanks go home Result of terrorist activity in London.

Yard A measure greater than the metre in every respect but length.

Yard, Prison A share-traders' impromptu meeting-place.

Yardstick A measure of quality, and therefore naturally associated with far-off pre-decimal days.

Ye Olde 1. Tourist trade pre-fix meaning '16th century pastiche' as in Ye Olde Tea Shoppe (Est. 1956), Ye Olde Filling Station, etc.
2. Elizabethan fore-runner of *The Oldie,* today's foremost geriatric style magazine.

Year of Living Dangerously Brussels view of twelve months spent eating warm custard tarts, unpasteurised cheese, and flavoured crisps, drinking tap-water, and buying bangers from butchers with sawdust on the floor.

Years, Advanced in What human civilisation doesn't really seem to have done.

Yellow belly Result of incorrect use of instant tan cream.

Yellow Pages Heavy telephone directory listing the numbers of TV repairers capable of mending set after heavy directory has been hurled at it in response to umpteenth repeat of ancient 'Yellow Pages' advert.

Yellow peril See 1. Wheel-clamp. 2. Egg yolk.

Yeoman, Stout Bumper box of freeze-dried instant mashed potato.

Yes and no Two of the shorter, less-favoured answers available to politicians for use in interviews.

Yob Defined by his social and intellectual superiors as someone who, like them, reads The Sun and watches satellite porn, but without their sense of ironic detachment.

Yoga Hindu mind-clearing exercises, akin to watching TV without a TV set.

Yoghurt See 'Yogourt'.

Yogourt See 'Yogurt'.

Yogurt Fast becoming the only culture devoured in the average home. See also 'Yoghurt' and 'Yogourt'.

York, Duke of Had 10,000 men. Or was that the Duchess?

Youthful in appearance Militant Oldie's code for 'stupid-looking'.

Yugoslavia The former name for what is now known as 'The Former Yugoslavia'.

Yule log Complex tax and VAT records kept by Father Christmas.

Zeal Aquatic mammal found off the Somerset coast.

Zebra A bar-coded horse.

Zigzags Road-markings placed either side of zebra-crossings to indicate to drivers that portion of road in which they should accelerate in order to avoid having to stop for pedestrians.

Zoetrope Device producing an illusion of movement. See also 'M25'.

Zzzzzz 1. Onomatopoeic representation of the buzz in the House of Lords. 2. Author and illustrator after finally finishing 'Dictionary'.

Dictionary for our Christmas-Time

Advent Popularly supposed to be a corruption of 'advert'.

A dog is for life, not just for Christmas Message not heeded in South Korean restaurants.

Batteries not included 1. True of every electrical toy with the exception of all those that make loud and irritating noises. 2. State of hearing aid shortly after unwrapping of toy in 1.

Cards Given to surplus employees the Friday just before Christmas.

Christmas Box Worse than usual TV.

Christmas Eve The Sun's December 24th Page 3 girl.

Christmas is Coming . . . First line of children's traditional rhyme, now updated to read: 'Christmas is coming/The goose is getting fatty/Time to rip his liver out/And make it into paté.'

Christmas, Old-fashioned The 'traditional' Victorian-style Christmas to which the poor and homeless are condemned each year.

Christmas stocking Face-mask worn by Yuletide bank-robber.

Crisis at Christmas 1. Turkey not fully defrosted. 2. A charity for the homeless.

Decorations, Tacky The New Year's Honours List.

Deep and crisp and even Styles of pizza.

Eleven Lords-A-Leaping Previously-resting Upper House members at the mention of tea and mincepies.

Feast of Stephen *Radio Times* description of close-together Christmas repeats of *Jeeves and Wooster, Blackadder,* and *A Bit of Fry and Laurie*.

Festive The look of any sad item to which a scrap of tinsel has been stuck.

Fir Tree which keeps its leaves all year round except during Christmas.

Four calling birds A quartet of MP's so-called 'research assistants'.

I Saw Three Ships Come Sailing In Carol still unpopular amongst Falkland Island residents.

January sales The highest monthly figures for indigestion tablets.

Jingle bells 1. To be replaced from 1998 by a standardised two-tone siren in accordance with EU directive X.379.2/c.

Manger, Away In A Franglais for 'Gone to Lunch'.

Mulling Name given to the process in which, by the addition of cloves and nutmeg, and the gentle application of heat, cheap red wine is made to taste even more revolting.

My Husband and I Cliché of royal speech more than ever associated with HM The Queen nowadays as she's about the only one still left with a spouse.

Nine Pipers Piping All that's left of the Band of the Black Watch after further military spending-cuts.

No Room At The Inn Result of increase in pub popularity after Christmas hits karaoke-machine installed.

Roast Turkey What Germany's growing band of neo-Nazis would seemingly like to do.

Santa's Little Helper Amphetamines.

Season's Greetings 'Get out of my way, I'm in a hurry!' 'I saw that parking-space first!' 'Been drinking have we, sir?' etc.

Sherry, British The only alcoholic drink legally obliged to carry a drawing on its label of a Victorian coach and horses.

Snowman, The Raymond Briggs's frozen asset.

Star of Wonder, Star of Light, Star of Royal beauty, bright Princess Diana, leaving aside the 'bright' bit, of course.

Xmas The tasteless typesetter's Christmas.

XXXXmas The tasteless lager drinker's Christmas.

Zzzzz Around 4 pm on December 25th.

MIKE BARFIELD was born in Leicester in 1962, and has worked extensively as a humorous writer for radio, TV, books, and the press. His credits include *Spitting Image*, *Punch, Private Eye, The Times, The Daily Telegraph, The Guardian, The Independent*, the London *Evening Standard*, and *The Beano's 'Dennis the Menace and Gnasher' Show*. He also produced and presented a show for satellite television that nobody saw. Soon to be married, he lives in a pet-free flat in West London.

STEVEN APPLEBY was born in Northumberland in 1956. Trained at the Royal College of Art, his work has appeared in many newspapers and periodicals including *Punch, Tatler, The Guardian, The Times, The Sunday Telegraph* and *Harper's and Queen*. He also wrote and illustrated the books *Men – The Truth, Normal Sex* and *Miserable Families*, to name but a few. He lives in south London, with his wife, two cats, three children, a canary, some rabbits, and an infinite number of cockatiels.

BARFIELD and APPLEBY first met at a *Punch* lunch in 1989. They next met at an *Oldie* lunch several years later. Since then they have eaten many types of meal together, and produce the ever-popular *In My Day . . .* strip for *The Oldie*.